My World:
Jump in Anytime!

Susan T.A. Sakelos

PublishAmerica
Baltimore

© 2004 by Susan T. A. Sakelos.
All rights reserved. No part of this book may be reproduced, stored in a retrieval system or transmitted in any form or by any means without the prior written permission of the publishers, except by a reviewer who may quote brief passages in a review to be printed in a newspaper, magazine or journal.

First printing

ISBN: 1-4137-2945-2
PUBLISHED BY PUBLISHAMERICA, LLLP
www.publishamerica.com
Baltimore

Printed in the United States of America

Dedication

My four precious sons fill my world with happiness and my heart with joy:
    Vincent Caprino
    Thomas Caprino
    Colby "Cole" Martin
    Casey Martin

My parents, Thomas and Florence. have a lot of love to give, and their sacrifices allowed me to become the person I am today.

The man I adore, who stood by me, inspired me and believed in me: Ralph Giordano

Do you remember *The Little Engine That Could?* The talking train would repeat to himself: "I think I can, I think I can." I have a family that repeatedly has told me: "I know you can."
    My aunts and uncles:
    Tootsie and Tony (Aceste)
    Ellen and Ron (Mackey)
    John (Sakelos)

The Fontana, Sakelos, Mackey, Pena and Gagliardi families are pieces of my heart that form completeness in me.

Acknowledgements

When I needed to give this book a title it became a huge task. I was given nine months to name each of my sons and still could have had more time. I asked a friend to help me and she did more than that—she titled the book. Many thanks to Phyllis Hershkowitz

My ego boosters: My cousin, Jerry Gagliardi, and my dear friend, Robert Durst. Both men took the time to show an interest and had confidence in me.

Mom and Pop—Thank you so much for the countless hours of listening to: "So, what do you think?"

> "The only things that count in life are the imprints of love which we leave behind us after we are gone."
>
> —Albert Schweitzer

Through these pages you will read a collection of experiences through the eyes of different generations. Each portion of my writing compilation is a variety demonstrated through a journal segment, an essay, a poem or a quote. There is a moral to the dozens of issues and experiences addressed in this publication. Each day we are subjected to experiences and rarely take notice of the lessons to be learned. Memories are manufactured daily and we tend not to realize the impact that one day can have on any one individual. Memories are made with each breath we take in our lives. The most important part of our encounters is what we have acquired from them to improve our outlook on life and collect memorable moments to treasure.

Experiences can take on a positive view. There is not an age limit determined on absorbing new knowledge.

When I concluded my memoirs, reality is…Life is a fast ride. Enjoy!

Table of Contents

Siblings	15
Only Child Syndrome	19
Only Five	25
Lacking Attention	28
The Little One	30
Haiku	35
Fishing	39
Baseball	45
On the Field	49
Phobophobia	51
Pets	57
A Colleague	65
The Yacht Party	69
An Hour Meeting	72
Go to Work vs. Stay at Home	75
A Visit to the Mall	77
An Astrology Lesson	83
Commuting Can Be Amusing	87
An Airport Experience	90
Fish in the Sea	95
Dreams, Nightmares or Daydreams	101
Children at Play	107
Unconditional Love	113
Wedding Bands	117
Technology	123
Soldier	126
Fame	129
Lightning Bug Fun	137
The Power of Love	145
Hope	151

The Fortune Teller	155
Media	159
Media Influence	165
Golden Rules	169
A Good Day is When…	173

"Twenty years from now you will be more disappointed by the things that you didn't do than by the ones you did do. So throw off the bowlines. Sail away from the safe harbor. Catch the trade winds in your sails. Explore. Dream. Discover."

—Mark Twain

Siblings

When I was growing up, I had no idea that I was missing a bond that so many others share. It is the special bond between siblings. During my adolescent years I can recall a friend of mine screaming at the top of her lungs and expressing the deep hatred she possessed for her sister. Of course her sister was doing the same thing at the same exact time, so it was obvious that I was happy to be an only child. It seemed to me that all my childhood friends hated their siblings, and I could not grasp the screaming concept. If my mother had heard me screaming in my room, she should have worried. An only child should never scream: "Let go, it's mine." Who would be my competitor? An only child is not necessary lonely but different. There was no competition nor screaming. The only screaming would be if my mother were expressing herself.

The greatest disadvantage would have been the fact that I had no one to place the blame on and could never point the finger at someone other than myself. As a child my home never heard the echoing words: "He did it!" "She did it!" Who could I blame when things broke? Who could be the victim of my destructiveness? How often could I blame my dog before my parents would feel the family dog (my only adopted sibling), had overstayed her welcome? I didn't want to relocate my dog to another family, so I couldn't blame her for breaking a vase.

That dog I grew up with was the perfect sibling for me. She obeyed my every command, never borrowed anything nor broke any of my toys. My dog, Demetria, a huge German Shepherd, was the sister I never had. Her patience had allowed me to polish her nails and she always had a pretty aroma from my perfume. I was an eight-year-old who believed I did not need a sibling. I was a very imaginative child and never realized that Demetria and I lacked conversation. I did all the talking and she did the listening. It was perfect for me. (You'll find as you read on how this treatment of animals haunts me in my adulthood.) At some point in my life I truly believed family pets were beneficial for a healthy and happy home.

It was only until I had children of my own that I realized what was absent from my childhood. I had an unknown void in my life. The short, sweet sentences of affection, "I hate you," translate into "I love you," in the adult form. I did not grow up with the other words that are used in my home today. Once again, the short sentences: "Don't touch me." "Leave me alone." "Give it back." "Is it yours?" The most habitually used, "Mine!"

All the chaos I missed in the past, I have made up for the lost time with my four sons.

The greatest gift I can ever give my boys, I have already given: the gift of one another…their siblings. They are so unsuspecting of the gift. One day they will know how fortunate they are to have one another.

> Children are likely to live up to what you believe of them.
>
> —Lady Bird Johnson

Only Child Syndrome

I live in an active home and we need to keep in mind that I did grow up as an only child. I do necessitate some special time and it is the short sound of silence. I enjoy quiet time (on occasion), and feel that I warrant some time and appreciate that time more than most people can imagine. The need for the calm silence, I have always called this Only Child Syndrome. This syndrome occurs when you need to use the bathroom and you always find someone occupying that space and they are taking their time in that room. The person before you in the bathroom decides to take a bath. The child you brought into this world proceeds to fill the tub to the top and use all the hot water or maybe they just leave the shower running continuously. The outcome is always the same…that cold water awaits you. Then when they exit the bathroom you hear: "Wow, that was great, I feel great. Oh, are you waiting to get in the bathroom?" With no expression, I look at my child and ponder if he thinks he lives alone. The next thought that intrudes into my mind is if he used soap because he certainly didn't use a towel. I do have a recollection of hygiene conversations in the past. I hear myself often scream: "Use soap!" I hope for the best. He walks out with his shirt and boxers adhering to his body and tries to convince me that he dried his body before clothing himself.

My five-year-old uses soap and it is confirmed by the bubbles that are still attached to his body when he steps out of the tub. He throws a towel around his shoulders (not his body just his shoulders) and takes tiny steps out of the bathroom. He needs to take tiny steps from the bathtub because he must keep his balance through the trail of puddles he is creating along the floor. He stands naked and looks up at me and announces: "I'm done. It was a freezin' hot bath." My eyebrows do most of the talking after that statement. My eyebrows suggest I sense confusion in his statement. I decide not to question him about the water temperature. I know the answer would be: "The water was hot and now I'm freezing." Young children give common sense answers that often leave you speechless. I try to ask very few questions.

This Only Child Syndrome strikes when you open the cabinet to indulge in your favorite cupcake and find the box empty. An empty box placed back in the cabinet. This is baffling and just another tiny dilemma. Then I look at this empty box in my hands and realize that this never happened to me as a kid. Perhaps because I was the only kid in the house and chances are I would have been in trouble and I had no one to blame. So the vacant box in my hands will remain a mystery and I am not indulging in my cupcake that I had intentions of enjoying. I have adjusted to these diminutive inconveniences, so when I open the refrigerator door, I am no longer puzzled to witness a two-liter bottle of soda that contains about one tablespoon of liquid just layering the depths of the bottle.

I try not to analyze any behavior, actions or situations in my home. It wastes time, and the likelihood of permanent change is really not possible. I am very well adjusted and now accustomed to the habits of my children. I now look back and realize they have given me memories that I cherish and hold so

MY WORLD: JUMP IN ANYTIME!

dear to my heart. Years from now I will miss the empty boxes in the cabinet and empty containers in the refrigerator. I know I will yearn for the chaos one day. I am ecstatic that I am outnumbered and those brothers will mature with very fond memories of their youth.

> The greatest mistake you can make is to be constantly fearful you will make one.
>
> —Unknown

Only Five

Kindergarten is the earliest traumatic experience that I can recall. If you were a child thriving for an education this class was certainly not a very good introduction. I can compare my kindergarten class to a military platoon and my class was contained in a huge room which I considered jail. I know this to be true because my teacher, Mrs. Berg, could have very well been a military leader or a jail warden. The truth (this really is the truth): my teacher had just returned to school from suffering *another* nervous breakdown. True story and what a great idea to let her teach the future generation.

Luckily for me, I was not easily intimated and it was distressing for Mrs. Berg. It was obvious that the parents of the children attending Mrs. Berg's class were never informed of her mental health status. It was brought to my mother's attention after *another* school visit. In the beginning of the adventurous education I was receiving, my mother would ask me if I had a good day. I always replied, "I had fun, and I played in the dol house all day." Little did my mother know that if you were *placed* in the dollhouse it was a punishment for talking. I did an excess of talking. I was an only child who took full advantage of surrounding myself with my peers and wanted to express myself among them. According to Mrs. Berg, who was molding the future generation, "You only speak if you are spoken to directly!" I heard this all day. All day.

Before I was aware of only child syndrome, I had some other disorder: "Talk-a-holism." Actually Mrs. Berg hoped I had the fear of words: *verbophobia*. I did not have any fear of words and used them constantly. I was the motor mouth of my class. Okay…maybe the entire school. I was a talkaholic and later would come home with notes pinned on my shirt. I would hear, "Susie, please come up to the front." (I knew I wasn't going to see her to receive a pat on the head. My lips moved, she knew my lips moved and I was in trouble.) There would be Mrs. Berg, waiting with a little white paper and a pin. The note would state that I needed to keep quiet. Mrs. Berg was known for affixing notes onto children's shirts with pins instead of placing the notes in school bags. If there were a tournament based on what student had the majority of notes attached to their clothing, I would have had the victory, hands down.

When I returned back home from a brutal day of kindergarten, I didn't want to remove my jacket. My mother would always rectify the situation and she was always the understanding mother. My mother standing in front of me was waiting for me to take off my jacket. My mother would say to me, "Well, give me your jacket." I stood there with a smile on my face and wouldn't give a reply. I wanted her to be proud that I didn't have a note pinned to my shirt. I did have another note attached. The result of this episode landed my mother back in school for yet another meeting.

My mother was able to handle the situation and all seemed fantastic for a while. Just for a short time. Mrs. Berg ultimately was able to shatter my spirit. She succeeded in bringing me to tears. It was Columbus Day and we had to make a picture of the *Nina*, *Pinta* and *Santa Maria*. I couldn't wait to finish my artwork and show my parents my ships. Well, once you completed your artwork, you proceeded to the front of the class, showed your completed project to the teacher and you'd receive a sticker (a reward) for the good job you had done. I was done with my "masterpiece" and brought it to her to receive credit. Mrs. Berg looked upon my ships with disgust and ripped them up in front of my five-year-old eyes, threw the pieces in the garbage next to her feet and spoke heartbreaking words: "This is horrible. You did it wrong. Go sit down." I can't recall why or how it could have been completed incorrectly. My ships may have been glued too close to each other. I may have used the wrong colors to complete my ships. If I had the 64-count box of crayons, I used all 64 colors.

I held up commendably until the doors of school opened. My classmates all poured out down the stairs with their ships in their hands. My mother had bent down to her knees to look at my watery eyes and asked: "Susie, where are your ships?" Unessential to say that was my mother's final trip to the teacher and Mrs. Berg's final year teaching. The irony was I decided to study art and art history in college. For years I wanted to mail Mrs. Berg photos of the *Nina*, *Pinta* and the *Santa Maria*, every Columbus Day, just to drive her crazy....I thought it to be unsuccessful since she had reached that point years ago.

I did go home at the end of that school year with one final note. My memory does not serve on the precise words, but it was a positive note on my progress.

If a child informs you that they had a rough day at school…believe it. Remember that all is possible. A five-year-old can have a bad day.

Little people. Little problems.

Lacking Attention

An only child is not always receiving attention. It is true that an only child doesn't have competition, but at times an only child can still feel ignored.

A dreary autumn weekend is quite a long weekend without siblings. I was 13 years old, my friends were nowhere to be found and I was really bored. What did I do? I moped around. I went to the refrigerator knowing that I was not hungry; I opened the door and closed the door. My father was watching television in the living room while my mother had the phone to her ear as she continued to cook. No one else seemed bored. I threw a toy to my dog and her eyes slowing moved up to meet my eyes. Her eyes were saying—*You don't really think I'm gonna get up and play*. I was getting more frustrated because I was on the pay-no-mind list in my family.

Because I wanted both parents (and the dog) to hear me, I announced loudly: "No one cares if I am here or not! I'm home and I go unnoticed!"

My mother hung up the phone to reassure me that my existence was crucial to the family and I was the most important issue to her and my father. It would have been more believable if she hadn't started walking back to the kitchen as she was reciting such kind words. Even better, if my father had said

MY WORLD: JUMP IN ANYTIME!

something more than "Shh" while watching *Gunga Din* on the tube for the hundredth time. As I passed the television set I sarcastically said: "Oh, Pop, I hope you didn't miss an important part." I headed up the stairs to my room and slammed the door behind me. Then I heard my father: "Damn it! Florence, your daughter is slamming doors!" I heard no response and everyone seemed happy returning to his or her interests. After about 30 minutes of me just lying on my bed, I got an idea. I had a plan. It was a test.

I would jump from the window onto the terrace, then proceed to climb down the side of the house and ring the bell. I gave it a go. I safely made it to the cement ground and went to the front door. I rung the bell. (We had a buzzer to open the door.) The door was not locked, but my mother pressed the button and the sound of the buzzer was heard. I walked in. My mother said: "Hi, honey."

Wow. I thought to myself, *Hi, honey*. My father was still watching the classic on the tube and I had to question my mother: "I was missing. Isn't it odd I would ring the bell to the home I live in? Didn't you know I was in my room?" I explained the test to her and she began laughing. Then I realized how "crazy" I made her at times.

She raised me to be independent and she never treated me any different than a family of six children. She was to make sure I was never referred to as "the spoiled only child."

That episode was a couple of decades ago and each passing year I understand her more. I have great parents. They had a tough job. They had me.

The Little One

My mother was the youngest of seven children and I would comment on the lack of attention she must have received. My mother did tell me that she and her siblings played hide-and-seek often. She was one of the siblings that was always hiding and not searching. She would hide and no one did seek. After a while she quit hide-and-seek because everyone enjoyed the game but her and that was understandable. She moved on to kick-the-can. I was an only child but luckily came of age with many cousins and I was the youngest. Sometimes no attention is better than the attention the littlest one will get. Some of us love to be scared and the others love to scare. If you are in a circle of individuals who love to scare and you are the youngest—you better believe you will become their victim.

I was just about seven years of age when I clearly remember celebrating a family member's birthday at my aunt's home in Brooklyn. Five of my cousins were there and it was decided that we could go play in the basement. I must have been a glutton for punishment. No matter what had transpired between us in the past, I still trusted my cousins. Why shouldn't I trust? We're blood. (A golden rule in our family.) I was excited to go play.

In the basement was a pool table and it seemed to be the big attraction. One of my cousins played around with the balloons.

MY WORLD: JUMP IN ANYTIME!

He hit it to me and I hit it back and so on. Another cousin came over to me and whispered in my ear, "Hear that?"
  I said pathetically, "What?"
  So we walked around and listened. Now we all were quiet and just listening. (For what I don't know.) Then one of the cousins said: "I think it's a cat." I didn't hear anything but still I traveled around quietly in the circle. Then I thought I heard a scratching noise. Maybe it was a cat and I adored animals. (My aunt didn't even own a cat at the time.) The lights were dim in the large basement and it was so quiet that you had been able to hear the lights humming. We all were standing in front of the closet, which just so happened was the dimmest area. There were sounds but I couldn't identify the noises.
  "Go ahead, Susie, open the door," my balloon-playing cousin whispered.
  I was a seven-year-old and my cousins were ten-year-olds and up. What is wrong with this picture? They were supposed to protect me. (I didn't think that way at the moment.)
  "Hurry up. It might be an animal in trouble," said my balloon-playing cousin.
  Now I was worried and without a second thought, I placed my hand on the doorknob and turned it open. At that moment Frankenstein was twice my height (although I think he was a giant back then), and his arms moved up from his sides to feel his way about. His hands were shaking fingers and searching for my little scrawny neck. My cousins were running around the basement screaming and tears were filling my eyes. Everyone was hysterical! I can't remember if any words escaped my mouth. After ten seconds one cousin started laughing. A few more seconds later everyone thought it was a big joke. My tallest cousin took off his Frankenstein mask and wanted to know if I liked his costume.

I don't remember speaking but I remember running up the stairs from the basement with intentions of giving up my family like a bad habit. The adults would only say, "Oh, Susie, they're just playing with you." I looked at my family as if they were crazier than my cousins, and in that case, I didn't want anyone to play with anymore if they were playing.

I seemed to get over the fright and the next scare date I planned to be more prepared. Many more scare dates did follow through our many years and I never really was prepared.

The old saying goes: Pick on someone your own size.

My personal moral: Pick on someone your own age.

> "Poetry is what gets lost in translation."
>
> —Robert Frost

Haiku

Throughout this book I have a variety of poetry. The most enjoyable and creative are Haiku poems. The art of Haiku is a traditional form of Japanese poetry. Each poem contains seventeen syllables and is designed to be three metrical units. These units are the three lines, the first of which contains five syllables, the second has seven and the third is a five-syllable line. That's just some extra information I have collected. A very good friend of mine, Phyllis, would encourage me and tell me on numerous occasions, "You have to write this stuff down."

So glad I took her advice. We don't agree on everything but we share a philosophical approach on life.

Unpredictable.
Life, a play, we share a part.
Drama. Comedy.

> If you ask a child to spell love, they would spell it: T-I-M-E
>
> —Unknown

Fishing

My five-year-old, Colby, whom we occasionally call Cole (our entire family will shorten everyone's name to one syllable), is a fisherman. Case (Casey) is a four-year-old that is happy doing anything with his three older brothers. I try very hard to accomplish family time. Fishing is a great way to enjoy family time and all four boys agree.

Fishing begins when we pack the van with all our fishing accouterment, snacks and coolers, then we jump in and head to the ocean. (This took a good hour just to organize.) Along the way we need to stop at the nearby bait and tackle shop to purchase the malodorous bait to catch "The Big One." We all agree to set free whatever we catch and never take life from the ocean. (I certainly do not need more pets in our home.)

When we arrive at "our spot" on the ocean's sand, we proceed to unpack. This takes a very, very long time. Everything we unpack needs to be inspected by the boys. It may be just a flying disc that they feel a need to throw around for short entertainment purposes. The beach ball must be treated the same as the flying disc. Now the cooler is open, everyone is thirsty from playing around the car and not one person has done anything productive in the last fifteen minutes. All of our fishing gear still remains inside the car.

The youngest two boys are chasing birds. Casey is very good at this sport. (It is a sport to Casey.) A bird is in sight, so Casey begins at a slow pace and then takes off faster than a rocket on his mission to capture the bird. Unfortunately for me, the bird is *running* along the sand. It is my luck that this bird is not flying, he's running. Casey is chasing the innocent bird along the ocean and he never turns back. Now, this is where my very own exercise program comes into play. He continues to chase a running bird and I chase Casey. I am so fatigued and the car remains unpacked. The second I get a hold of Casey's hand, the bird expands his wings and soars away. I shake my head continuously and turn back to the car with Casey in hand. I get to the car only to find the three boys are keeping themselves engrossed and all our gear is in the car. One is writing his name in the sand with a tree branch. Another is throwing peanuts in the air and trying to capture them with his mouth while the other is observing the sky. My son Tommy notices my return and then glances at me and asks, "What are we doing? Are we going to fish?" I can't help but glare at my four boys and excitedly but sarcastically say, "Hey, what a great idea!"

Most fishing stories are told with enthusiasm and powerful narration of the catch. Most fish tales contain the line: "My hands were shakin' and you couldn't believe his strength, he was putting up a real fight." I have also heard: "I couldn't even reel the line in by myself. That fish was so huge." All the fishing stories have the reel and the rod in mind, but not my family. Our family uses short sentences or questions: "Where's the hook?" "Who's got the bait?" "My line is tangled." And the last line is: "He hooked me." Our fishing stories make us laugh when we speak to others about our fishing day.

Vince (Vincent) and Tom (Thomas), my older sons, stare and wait for their lines to move. One hour feels the equivalent

MY WORLD: JUMP IN ANYTIME!

of five hours at an airport for the boys. Suddenly you hear: "I got 'em," the words spoken frantically from the mouth of a five-year-old. The entire family stares at Colby who is holding a tiny fish by its tail and Colby is wearing a huge smile. The older boys bought live bait and Cole caught bait right out of the storage bucket with his tiny hands. Cole caught the bait and he was so proud. Then again, it was the only catch of the day.

Baseball, A young man
remembers as a child
standing at the plate.

Walking to the plate
repeatedly his name heard
silence as he waits.

Lights glare from above.
The past, he often daydreams
now he stands a man.

The game through the years
You can't possibly outgrow
The love of the game.

— Susan Thomas Alexandria

Life affords no greater responsibility, no greater privilege, than the raising of the next generation."

— C. Everett Koop, MD

Baseball

A baseball field is my home away from home. I grew up with the sport my father adored. My father was a baseball player for the United States Navy. A third baseman in 1956, who had the love for the game in his heart. Anyone can see the passion for the game in his eyes when he reminisces the great moments of baseball.

It is many years later and God's will has my father teaching my sons the game just as he taught me in my childhood. I believe he has his work cut out for him. Teenagers know it all, and they have a special knack to make you feel as if you are wasting your time educating them. When my father corrects my sons, their eyes roll while the neck allows the head to roll back and they stare up to the sky. Now you repeatedly hear from the teenager's mouth that standard quote: "Yeah. Okay."

I step in to support my father, in my stern and serious voice. "You **better** listen and pay attention when your grandfather is speaking to you." I guess that is a threat. That type of threat continues to go unknown, but everyone says that and it seems to work for short periods of time. I now come to my own defense and support my own actions, insisting that I was never like that as a kid. Immediately upon stating I **was not** the know-it-all teenager, both my parents stare at me as if I were an alien with three heads and was just sent down to earth from another planet. They bring me back to reality just by bringing up *everything* I did as a kid. Challenging my parents is a mistake. I must have selective memory. (I obviously have passed this trait on to my children.) My mom reminds me, "Susie, the apple never falls far from the tree."

My oldest son was asked to wear his uniform and run onto the field of a minor league stadium. The stadium was beautiful and exactly the same as a major league stadium. The only difference between the two was the capacity of the crowd. Our neighborhood baseball league organized this and the kids loved the idea of their feet upon this enormous field. The boys would be announced individually by their names, numbers and their positions. The team would run out onto the field and take their given positions. Once the boys took their positions, our country's anthem would play.

The night was clear, the sun had just set over the ocean and the boys were on the field. The view was breathtaking. Minutes prior to the playing of our anthem, my father walked and stood next to me. His eyes were glassy from the tears that wallowed inside his eyes. I remember him saying to me: "I played in a stadium just like this one…just doesn't seem like it was so long ago."

I believe that tears are expressed with different emotions all at the same time. The clock never stops, time just moves along, and my father proudly watched his grandson. It is possible to feel young again through the eyes of a child. I just remember thinking at that moment how blessed my children and I were to have this special man as our gift. Not all fathers and grandfathers are gifts, but this man is a gift.

He gave us his heart.

> "How a person plays the game shows something of his character—how he loses shows all of it."
>
> —Unknown

On the Field

My four boys and I agree on baseball as well as fishing. God did not grant Vincent with patience. If he has any, no one knows. He stands in center field while the pitcher on his team is having a rough day. There hasn't been a batter that made contact with the ball, but bases are loaded. As the pitcher faces another batter my son has lost whatever patience he thinks he possesses. He starts to pace in a little space, impatiently jumps up and down a couple of times. The pitcher walks the next batter and a run is scored with no hits in the game. Now my son throws his hat to the ground, then he retrieves the hat from the dirt and places it back on his head. Another pitcher comes out to the pitcher's mound and eventually gets the team out of the inning.

Vincent saunters back to the dugout with a dirty team hat and he appears fatigued. My son pats the original pitcher on the shoulder and reassures him, "Come on. Get off that attitude. It's no big deal, everyone has a bad day." Was this the same kid I viewed in the outfield? He kept me amused and I then glance over at him and he just gives a smile as if the game just began. How quickly he forgot the time he just spent expressing his frustration in the outfield.

If my son Tommy is in the outfield during a long period of

time with no action, he can keep himself amused. God gave him a special gift. The gift of music. He is fortunate to be a musician who whistles his time away on the field. He also was granted the gift of patience. Tommy limits his worries. If he strikes out, he believes the next time up at bat will be the home run he well deserves.

Casey is too young to be part of any organization so he is Cole's support during the game. Cole wants to be a baseball player just like his big brothers. I informed my older boys that they really need to attend Cole's first game. Colby is looking forward to a crowd and his own cheering section.

Grandparents and brothers sit with me in the cheering section. Colby is up to bat. He stands at home plate and waits for his pitch. It only took ten pitches until he decided to swing. He hits the ball and everyone is screaming, "Run!" One coach is shouting: "Drop the bat. Run. Drop the bat." How much stress can a five-year-old endure? He is the last batter and he is supposed to run the bases till he reaches home plate. He passes first base and is heading toward second base, wearing a smile throughout the entire ordeal. Another coach is heard: "Colby, you have to touch the bases." My son took this literally. He turns back heading for first. He stops in front of the bag, bends down and touches the base with his hands. When he stands back up, he still wears a smile to express his accomplishment. He finds his cheering section in the crowd, raises his hand high and waves. Baseball at its best.

Phobophobia

I am fascinated with the concept of phobias. In the late 1700s the Greeks invented the word *phobia* to classify fears in general. Then came Latin, the language to introduce individual phobias. I have a difficult time understanding why each phobia needs a name. Psychologists and psychiatrists have spent countless hours on naming the large quantity of different phobias. The medical professionals determined that these phobias are classified as a mild psychological problem, and to be considered an anxiety disorder. This concept leaves me uneasy. If I appear to be doubtful of stepping inside a crowded train in New York City, it will only take one person to try and convenience me that I have a problem. They will tell me that it is not "normal" to avoid a crowded train and I should seek help. I then would have a consultation with a therapist, and I would be diagnosed with a phobia or some psychological issue. Plenty of work all because of a decision made not to enter the crowded subway. I will wave down a taxicab. Although, if I had patience and time available to kill, there would be some insurance company willing to pick up the expense of any psychological needs to help me with my commuting disorder.

Sigmund Freud was an Austrian physician who became the founder of *psychoanalysis*. He believed everything had to do with repression and sexual desires. The nature of the phobia did not matter to Freud. These phobias could be cured once you were able to uncover the hidden repressed feelings. It was all about your past and the need to confront the issue. Unlike Freud, there is the behavioral therapist that uses a technique called *systematic desensitization*. This method combines exposure to the fear gradually along with relaxation to reduce anxiety.

I believe what fascinates me the most is the countless hours spent on these phobias. I don't even know if I have any phobias. I don't fear growing old (*gerascophobia*), I just **don't want** to grow old. *Arachibutyrophobia* is the fear of peanut butter sticking to the roof of your mouth. The obvious cure would be to avoid eating peanut butter. I am really amazed that someone is in therapy for this phobia and a professional is going to help him or her cure this phobia at the expense of health insurance companies. Any wonder why the cost of medical coverage is not affordable?

Pronunciation is even a more astonishing task. I would've needed to take a special course in college: Pronunciation 101. If I were able to pronounce these words with little work involved, I would have used them at the office. I would no longer need to use a sick day. I would considered this a phobia day. It is known to be a medical condition. I have a difficult time spelling these phobias as well, an example: *chronomentrophobia*. How many syllables is that word?

The point I am trying to make is the convenience of stating "I fear clocks." If I called my boss and seriously explained that I am anemophobic and unable to get into the office, he may be taken by surprise or even sympathize with my phobia. It sounded so serious and professional. I am so lucky he has no phobia knowledge and that leaves me with the upper hand. I could call the boss and claim: "I fear wind." Not a very effective approach to get the day off from work. The proper name is effective: *anemophobic*. What could he do? Fire me? He would fear that I could take him to court and press charges that he is prejudiced against anemophobics. I win again.

Just to subject you to how far some people will go:

A man was on trial for murdering half a dozen beautiful women and decided his defense would be best if he blamed his crime on a phobia. This was his only defense since the evidence was overwhelming to convict this man. Caligynephobia is the fear of beautiful women and he was standing trial trying his best to convince a jury he didn't kill those innocent beautiful women. Someone should have explained to this man that if he really feared them, he would have been running away from the women at a freeway speed. His attorney should have explained to his client that a fear is something you avoid. He was convicted of murder and wasn't awarded any psychological treatment. Smart jurors. Phobias cause anxiety. Not crimes.

I am impressed with the dedication the medical professionals give to phobias. Speaking for myself: "Way too much work involved." I know of many phobias from a psychology class I needed to take in college. I have never had a need to use any of those fancy extravagant words. Until now. I tend to have a philosophical approach to many instances in my life. Not to the extreme. I am still trying to solve the biggest issue, the most mind-boggling…"What came first, the chicken or the egg?"

Life can be simple.

> Through a child's eyes,
> Empty house becomes home,
> When pets fill the space.

Pets

My kids are fortunate that I love animals and I am not *zoophobic*. (I feel the need to throw in some of these words throughout the book. I also need to feel I am still benefitting from my education.) Our family has had more than our share of family pets. Psychologists believe that children should own pets. It teaches them responsibility and a child can express himself to his pet. I guess it would be a special bond between them. Statistics show that adults live longer when they own a pet. According to psychologists, owning a pet is beneficial to all in the home.

Our home consisted (take notice: "consisted," past tense) of guinea pigs, iguanas, chinchillas, gerbils and hamsters. These pets did not live to their given life expectancies. We still have a cat, fish and one parakeet. These three pets are known to be the survivors. They may need their own psychologists, but nonetheless, they are survivors.

Our cat has been dressed appropriately for Halloween, has had the antlers placed on his head for Christmas and owns his very own big bunny ears for Easter. He has been the most photographed cat in history and owns a very impressive portfolio. Our cat's name is Vito and he has succumbed to each child in the house. He has been in boxes (imaginative spaceships), tubs (an imaginative ocean), and luckily never made his way into the laundry room. The laundry room would have been his very last adventure. Vito is the smartest of all animals. The kids walk toward him and he plays dead. This cat does not draw attention. He tries his best to go unnoticed.

Hamsters can die from internal injuries or even heart attacks at any age. Our hamsters lived on the edge by no choice of their own. The little critters were drag racing for much of their lives. They drove *remote-control* vehicles and their lives were placed in the hands of crazy operators. The cat has gave these furry friends plenty of stress. When I think about it, these furry friends we call hamsters have caused ME to have stress.

Our family had this one hamster for a very long time. (A long time spans for about two years.) While cleaning out the glass aquarium tank that was considered his living quarters, his glass home shattered and he needed to relocate. At that moment I did not have extra hamster homes. I placed the hamster in the tub, closed the drain, shut the bathroom door and considered him safe till I bought a new cage at some point during that day. Ralph, a man I consider my soulmate, decided he would help me out of this minor dilemma. He would pick up a new cage and drop it off to the house.

I was busy cleaning up glass, it was the summer and everyone was home running in and out of the house and I forget about the homeless hamster. At least until I noticed the bathroom door open. I entered the bathroom and reluctantly peered into the tub. No hamster. Frantically I searched for the furry creature. (He was only a few inches long, not very strong and it was not possible for him to make an escape from the bathtub.) The cat stood tall in the middle of the kitchen. I stopped dead in my search and stared at the cat. He dropped the lifeless hamster out of his mouth. By that time, everyone was searching for the hamster. I quickly swept the saliva-covered hamster off the floor and threw him in a paper towel and inside a small clear plastic bag.

The phone rang during the chaos at my home. I answered the phone, still holding the plastic bag, telling the older boys to call off the search. On the other end of the phone I hear Ralph explaining the cage he had just purchased. The man had the day off from his prestigious company in the corporate world and his one day off was spent shopping for pet cages. (I am sure he will think twice about taking another day off from his position.) He was holding a new cage and I was holding the dead hamster. He started explaining the cages, and told me he had purchased the duplex instead of the condo cage. In a few words, I told him that I had a dead hamster. His only response was: "Okay. Do I return the cage or am I supposed to fill it?" (He has been exposed to the craziness that lies inside my home and he continues his association with all of us. Very brave man.) I told him to bring the cage to me and I would buy a replacement later. My very good friend, Carmela, became the replacement lady. She took over filling the cage.

That was one of many episodes involving hamsters. Today we do not own any hamsters because I believe owning those critters will shorten my life expectancy. Stress is a killer.

We own very smart fish. I consider them smart because they are still living. Casey enjoys fishing in the tank, but he has never caught any of our fish. Casey is also in charge of feeding the fish. He on occasion thinks that they are famished and feeds them an overabundance of food. The fish are aware that gluttony is a common cause of death among fish. We have smart fish. They have never tried to consume all the food floating around in their water. I never gave fish very much credit for intelligence. They proved me wrong.

Casey loves animals. His goal is to give animals love. Simple. Colby feels that each will be his equal. His very own playmate. We own a parakeet and I remember Colby staring at the parakeet for quite some time. Colby looked at me and sighed. Then I heard him say: "Don't you feel bad for him? He has no hands." I explained that he had wings to enable him to fly. I also had rules that the parakeet could never leave his cage because he would fly away. Colby decided that taping his wings would be a good idea. The parakeet would be so happy that he could leave his cage and not fly away. Fortunately I witnessed his plan in action and grabbed the tape from Cole before any suffering occurred.

If any person gives a parakeet time and patience, it can learn to speak. An example: you repeatedly say "Hello" about half an hour daily, and the bird will learn to repeat it in a few weeks. We never spoke to our parakeet on a daily basis but our telephone rings constantly. Unfortunately for me, our phone is next to the parakeet's cage. Now I have a phone and a parakeet that ring.

After years of owning pets and still having more than the average family, Colby still insists on owning bugs. One day in August, Colby decided he needed a bug. He found his jug and made a little home for his helpless victim. Very excited, he announced: "I am looking for bugs. Come on, help me." I am not happy with the sport of catching bugs. Pet stores do not sell bug food and that leads me to believe they are not to be considered pets. God made bugs for outdoor purposes. God made bugs to spoil your appetite at a picnic or a barbecue. They are not for indoor use.

So, I was on the hunt for bugs even though it was not in my interest. I put it off that it was a learning experience and it wouldn't be Cole's career. By a neighborhood tree he had crouched down with his cup in hand. A huge, ugly ant was moving at top speed from the dirt onto the concrete. I heard his cup slam against the concrete and in a confident voice Colby stated, "I got him." (He says that repeatedly.) I watched him move the ant into his new home. Colby was very excited. He was already thinking of a name for the petrified ant. I am not a pet psychologist, I am not a trained professional, but I can diagnose an ant. That ant feared humans. That ant had the fear of children (*pedophobia*).

The ant and Colby were buddies. Colby talked to the ant constantly and the ant would listen because Cole insisted he was a good listener. This ant's days were numbered since the moment of his capture, and the day came when the ant was no longer moving about in his home. I could have explained to Colby that he was sleeping, and I would go ant hunting for a replacement without his knowledge. I decided to explain the death situation to the five-year-old. The speech did not last very long because I was interrupted right after I began speaking. He was sitting on the steps outside our home with the bug on his lap and I sat down next to him.

I started, "Colby, no one lives forever."

Colby interrupts, "I know."

Colby was still staring at the bug as I explained the process of going to heaven to live with God for eternity. He was still staring at his lifeless friend. I felt he was ignoring me. Finally I said to Colby, "Why are you still staring at him? He is not going to move, he is dead."

Colby finally turned his head to me, looked at me as if I were such a pathetic soul and he was the authority on death. He finally said to me, "Watch him or you are going to miss it."

So there we were both sitting on the steps with a dead bug upon his lap. I patiently sat with him and prayed that he didn't require funeral services for his eighth-of-an-inch friend. I had to ask him, "Why are we staring at him?"

Right before he answered my question, I thought I had done a fairly good job explaining death to him and the afterlife process. So sincerely, my child answered me: "We are watching and waiting for him to go to heaven." My son was waiting for him to float into the sky and eventually disappear.

I have learned that kids are literal. I also know the procedure following the death of a pet living in captivity. The procedure involves getting the pet out of his cage quickly and quietly. It will appear that the pet made the journey to the white pearly gates in the sky.

As I grow older, it will come as no surprise if I am diagnosed with zoophobia.

(*Guess I should have introduced the 1970s' "Pet Rock" to my kids.*)

> "I have said nothing because there is nothing I can say that would describe how I feel as perfectly as you deserve it."
>
> —Kyle Schmidt

> "Tell me who admires you and loves you, and I will tell you who you are."
>
> —Charles Augustin Sainte-Beauve

A Colleague

When I first graduated from college, I began working for an advertising firm. Working for that firm, I learned more about life and people rather than advertising experience. I was 21 years old and part of the 1980s, when more women were entering the "man's world." The era I define as *The Battle of the Sexes*. Not only did the competition take place in the corporate world, but in city blue-collar workers as well. More and more women went to work regardless if they had children. I did not have any offspring at the time and was just planning on marriage and wedding arrangements for later in that year. My coworkers appeared excited for me and wished me all their best. Well...not Harry.

Harry and I had our offices facing each other by no choice of our own. He would look at me and shake his head, not understanding the marriage concept. After a few weeks, he finally approached me. I assumed his neck started to hurt from all that shaking back and forth when he would glare my way. Harry stood in front of my desk and questioned, "Why make one man happy, when you could make many happy?"

He left me speechless. I remembered asking him if it was just a compliment or an actual question that required an answer.

He just walked away from my desk and out my office door.

When I resigned from the company a year later, I remember the last thing Harry said to me, "You are unaffected by your beauty. Always keep that quality." He and I never spoke customarily, but if he had something to say, it was usually a powerful statement. Harry gave me the definition of quality and quantity of words. He chose quality.

A man of few words.

The following is dedicated to my advertising friends:

> Advertising may be described as the science of arresting the human intelligence long enough to get money from it.
> —Unknown

> Never say no when a client asks for something, even if it is the moon. You can always try, and anyhow there is plenty of time afterwards to explain that it was not possible.
> —Richard Nixon

> Everyone is allowed an occasional failure—except the skydiver, of course.

> "Going to work for a large company is like getting on a train. Are you going sixty miles an hour or is the train going sixty miles an hour and you're just sitting still?"
>
> —J. Paul Getty

The Yacht Party

A career in advertising requires the meeting of deadlines, creating new concepts for your clients' ads, working with many different companies at the same time and working with outside freelancers. I worked for a New York agency and the stress level was considerably high but the benefits were grand. The benefit of socializing. After all, our company was giving business to printers, photographers, newspapers, magazines and even radio stations. When they had parties, we had parties. They hosted parties, we attended.

Invitations were not limited to the holiday season; we attended all year round. Someone, somewhere, was celebrating something. Our company received an invitation for a *Forbes* party. We had placed ads in *Forbes* magazine and we received four invitations to represent our advertising agency. I eagerly accepted the invitation along with my three coworkers. They were actually friends, not just coworkers, and this made our company desirable. The party would take place aboard the *Forbes* yacht. I was very enthusiastic—I would be surrounded by the "prestigious people" in the business world. I was always eager to absorb new knowledge from others with experience.

I remember the weather, very little humidity, and the party was to start promptly at six that August evening. I was tardy.

That was bad. (You can run behind schedule when attending a party that is stationary, but not a party that is mobile.) Christopher, one of the three coworkers, called my cellular phone from the yacht and calmly asked, "Susan, where are you? I am trying my best to stall the individual holding the guest list. They are ready to leave."

I was still scrambling to get there and I responded, "Keep him busy with conversation, get him a drink and keep repeating to him, 'She'll be here any minute' and one of those minutes I will appear."

I was almost there, I was approaching my destination. I stepped out of the taxi and all I needed to do was walk down the street a bit and cross over to the other side of the West Side Highway. I was unable to get to the corner to cross. The heel of my shoe had found the grating in the cement sidewalk. My heel was stuck, but I obviously needed my shoe. I called Christopher and stressfully explained, "I am just yards away, I am in the process of rescuing my shoe." Christopher had known me long enough to know that anything was possible, and if something outrageous could happen, it would to me. I returned my cellular phone to my purse. I needed to take my foot out of my shoe, bend down, then tug until I freed it. I was trying to envision what everyone who was witnessing the dilemma might be thinking. Cars were passing, people were walking and my skin tone was becoming a brighter red as the seconds passed.

I was wearing a very attractive dress and I was now on my knees over the city's grating. Marilyn Monroe stood over metal slats wearing a sexy white dress and the breeze from below ground ran up her legs making her dress flair. Marilyn was a voluptuous sex symbol—I was far from appearing sexy, fun and seductive; after all, I was on my knees, fighting with my shoe that was winning the bout. I was getting attention that I really didn't need at that moment. What would people think as they passed by in their cars? Finally, it was free. The entire ordeal took place in a few short minutes, although it felt like an eternity.

The positive aspect of the ordeal was the fact that the heel was still attached to the shoe. I placed the shoe—with an overabundance of scratches—back on my foot and began to step around the metal slats and wait for the light to change. I glanced over to take notice of a few useless construction workers who had watched from about 15 feet away. While glaring at the men, I questioned: "So, you boys were entertained watching the shoe saga?" I started crossing the street with a mission, not waiting for the men to answer my question. I made it across a busy Manhattan highway without falling or tripping, and I was still wearing the pair of shoes. I boarded the *Forbes* yacht. The impossible was reality. I had made it.

Everything was exquisite. The hunter green décor, the superb butler and maid service, the top deck exhibiting the *Forbes* aircraft, and a breathtaking sunset added to the magnificence. After an hour of flowing conversation and cocktails, I felt the need to have a quiet moment on the deck. The crisp air felt in a summer breeze carried the ocean's scent and was a small element of that moment aboard the yacht. We sailed in the darkness passing the New York skyline and the Statue of Liberty. At that moment, standing on the deck, I knew that all aboard were omitting the very best part of that evening. My mission was accomplished.

We take for granted. We need to take notice.

An Hour Meeting

It was a beautiful spring day and I was running behind schedule. I had dropped the kids at school and I was late for a meeting at work. I decided to drive my car rather than use public transportation. I looked at my gas tank, and as no shock to me, I needed to stop at the gas station. While my tank was filling I grabbed a cup of coffee and a newspaper at the station. Now I was ready to get to work. No sooner had I begun to drive and pick up a speed of 30 miles per hour, than traffic ahead was horrible. I slowed down and came to a stop. From that moment on, it would be bumper to bumper.

It is never a good time to drive in Manhattan, but at eight o'clock in the morning I consider it one of the worst times to drive. I needed to go to the theater district and luckily I was near my building. I found a parking spot. Most drivers never park on the street because of the time available on the meters. Each quarter you place in the meter's slot will give you 15 minutes to park with an hour time limit. Needless to say I had no quarters. Just when I thought that commuting was difficult—try to get change in New York. Stores will not make change unless you buy something. I could buy a pack of gum with my dollar and get a quarter change. I would need to do this four times because the meter required four quarters. By the time I obtained the correct amount of quarters, I would have received a ticket. The city of New York has employees that know empty meters. I decided to ask people walking by, and although everyone tries to be helpful, they aren't unless they have change. Finally—someone out there had change. He was my hero for the day.

I only had an hour on the meter and I would get change in my office and then return in an hour to replenish the meter. I knew the meeting would only run about an hour and everything was under control. I was finally in my building, and I stepped into the elevator and the doors closed. The elevator was express to the thirty-third floor. I was fumbling through my papers and putting my folders in order. I realized that I was organizing for a long time and I was still on the elevator. I tried to remember if the doors opened and I wasn't paying attention. I realized that an engineer was what I needed right about then. I pushed the sound alarm button and immediately heard a voice from the elevator intercom. The voice said, "Can I help you?"

I thought to myself, *He must be kidding. I didn't ring the bell to just say hello!* I replied, "I'd like to get out of the elevator. I am not moving."

He asked me if I could wait a minute—as if I had any choice in the matter. Then he proceeded to tell me that I was moving, but because of mechanical difficulty the elevator was moving very slow.

What did he expect me to say? I sarcastically responded, "Okay, guess I'll wait."

I reached my company's floor. I went to the conference room and my boss had that angry look in his eye but continued to smile in the company of our clients and quietly questioned me: "Where the hell have you been?"

I sincerely answered him, "In the elevator."

We ended our private whispering conversation and got to work. The meeting was a success. I constantly checked the time and got one of my coworkers to put change in my meter. I prayed she deposited the change in my meter and not the one directly outside. My meeting was over and I just wanted to go home. I was standing near the elevators and avoided the one which I had come up on. I stepped into the elevator and it worked. Things were looking up. I stood outside my building near the curb and stopped a minute to appreciate the weather. Standing next to me was a uniformed man writing out a summons and writing the car information on the ticket. He looked at me and started to justify his actions. "I hate doing this. I really feel bad but there are rules we have to follow. Everyone should check on their meters." He was going on and on with explanations. It sounded like the preaching my father had given to me in the past and actually still does today. When the man was done with his words of wisdom, I turned to him and said, "Well, I am so glad I have time left in my meter." He looked at me as if I had disillusioned him. I never once said that it was my car; I was only standing next to it.

I walked to my car and noticed that five cars were parked on the block and three of those cars had tickets on them.

I had beat the odds! That day was a success!

Go to Work vs. Stay at Home

    I moved on to another advertising agency. I did learn about advertising and about people during my employment at that agency. That job allowed for socializing with our company's clients. Most clients had one thing to accomplish: the need to overpower other's success. When attending an office function, the self-absorbed clients tended to speak of their accomplishments.
    I was expecting my first son in the early summer of 1989. There had been a question directed to me prior to my son's birth and was repeated constantly: "When will you be returning to the office?" Three months was the usual maternity leave time. Just recently, mothers were expected to return in six weeks. I was uncertain of my future plans and always feared explaining why I would not return. Most career-oriented people could not understand the staying-at-home-and-raising-the-child concept. I knew my first priority and only concern was to raise and enjoy my offspring. Our beginning stages race by so quickly and I wanted to participate in my child's youth. What would everyone say once I proposed my staying-at-home plan?
    This fear finally vanished when a colleague of mine brought his wife to an office Christmas party. My colleague's wife, Anna, was a mother and housewife. Many others could not believe

that it was a job until she decided to explain her typical day to a client at the party. The famous question: "What do you do?" Very vague question but everyone knows exactly what is implied in question. A client approached Anna and gave the standard question: "What is it *you* do?"

My colleague's wife answered without any hesitation: "It's funny you should ask. I was just imagining switching places with you because I really need a break. Let's see—I run a laundromat, I am chef, a postal worker, a gardener, an accountant. I also tutor. I provide custodian services as well as chauffeur services. I am a guidance counselor, but some days I use my nursing skills. I am on the board of directors for various sport councils, I enjoy doing some interior designing and in my spare time I freelance with my advertising and writing background." Anna never needed to take a deep breath until the end of her daily description. After Anna took in some air, she turned to continue speaking with the client who questioned how her days were spent. Anna curiously asked, "What is it *you* do again?"

Need I say more?

A Visit to the Mall

I try to avoid the shopping mall due to anxiety. It can be a stressful adventure. When I drive to the mall I have a goal. As soon as I open the door to enter the mall, I quickly head to the store where I need to make my purchase. I proceed to make my purchase and I am ready to exit the same door.

I have noticed that the mall is occupied with people that stroll around without a destination. A perfect analogy would be a park filled with people walking around aimlessly. Teenagers go to the mall and have an itinerary. They will meet their friends, grab a bite to eat, then walk around and meet new friends. It is the "hot spot" for the young teenagers. I figure that the mall serves a purpose and it functions as a transitional stage. These young kids go to consume food and socialize. It is the young "bar scene." There are some serious shoppers and you can tell because of the many bags they are holding and they appear fatigued. Then there are shoppers that aren't actually fatigued but annoyed by the non-shoppers who get in their way and slow down the shopping process.

I have witnessed all kinds of people while in a line in the center of the mall. I was in a long line for almost 40 minutes and was able to observe the crowd. It was the holiday season and I was waiting to visit Santa. Not just me, I brought my four sons along. I told my two oldest boys that I would take them to the mall for a bite to eat, and I conveniently left out the Santa visit. If I mentioned a Santa photo, my oldest child, Vincent, who could have been famished, would rather starve and would never walk in the mall with me.

I was focused on everyone at the mall trying to ignore the constant complaints from my four boys. All four voices were non-stop. Vincent would look down at the floor and nonchalantly glance about to make sure none of his teenage friends noticed him. He kept repeating, "I can't believe this. Really. I can't believe this." He was quite disgusted with the Santa trip. My second-born, Tommy, wanted to make me happy and didn't complain about the photo, but told me about his wish list. He is the kid who would tell Santa, "Wait, Santa, I have my laptop. Give me a minute to bring up my list on the screen." My third-born, Colby, was repeating, "Why is this taking so long? Are we getting closer? We aren't moving." His patience is very limited, but I distracted him by asking him to rehearse his wish list. This was the first year not one child was crying with fear and staring at Santa as if he were the most frightening human that had ever lived. My youngest, Casey, was excited for the first time and all that could be heard from his mouth was, "Ho, ho, ho. Santa, hi!" And he just kept waving. He began to wave with both hands as if he were practicing to become a politician in the future.

Just by standing in that long line, I felt good about myself. I was watching one child screaming, while another one was lying on the floor kicking, and another was clawing, biting and pulling at his mother's hair. Those parents were very determined to get their children on Santa's lap, and I felt so great I was not involved or participating with that form of torture. (I just have kids that talk as much as me. This was a

MY WORLD: JUMP IN ANYTIME!

spell my mother put on them for my payback. She was famous for informing me of the old saying: "What goes around, comes around.") If my child were exercising a tantrum, I would have left the line long ago without a problem. We moved up, getting closer. Finally, the moment we had all been waiting for...the visit to Santa and his huge chair. Santa looked worried when his visitors were taller than he was. Five of us stood in front of him and I told Santa that it wouldn't be painful and we would take a quick photo. The two little guys were on each knee and the two older guys were standing on each side. I did not join in for the picture; instead, I stood next to the photographer feeling so proud that we actually were successful with our adventure.

Then we paid ten dollars and waited for the elves to print our one 5x7 photo. The elf handed me the photo and the boys were in a huddle with me to view the photo. Each child of mine wore a smile the second they looked at the photo, so our Santa visit really was a success. It brought a smile to the faces of four young boys.

The next trip to the mall would be for another visit—the Easter Bunny would be hopping down the bunny trail soon enough!

> Stars, The sun, The moon.
> Wisdom in the sky above?
> Tales they tell, unknown.
>
> —Susan Thomas Alexandria

An Astrology Lesson

I do not know if any phobias exist when it comes to astrology. Perhaps psychologists and psychiatrists should perform a study. If and when there is a phobia listed in the phobia dictionary, I already know a woman that will cause others to acquire and then be diagnosed with this mental illness: the fear of astrology.

I was riding the subway in New York City and was sitting next to a woman in her mid to late forties. The perception that New Yorkers are unfriendly people is definitely a misconception. I was sitting on the train for two minutes before this woman started a conversation with me. It must have been within 60 seconds I knew her name was Lisa, she was recently divorced and worked in uptown Manhattan. I normally carry a conversation, but this woman never gave me a chance to cut in on the conversation. She talked enough to frighten a neighborhood bartender. She spoke enough to frighten me!

Finally she asked me a question so that I could do some talking as well.

"What's your sign?"

At first I thought she had spent too much of her time drinking at various bars and felt this was a good way to make conversation. I glanced at a book she held on astrology. I was curious about what she had to say so I answered, "Libra." One word is all I had in the conversation. I was hoping the question she asked would be more general rather than specific. General questions require extensive conversation.

Lisa continued explaining how I should follow my star sign in order to improve my life. I didn't think I needed to improve my life nor did I want to make any changes in my life at that moment in time. All I said to her was "Libra." I found out that because I am an air sign, I can only have an earth sign as my soulmate. If I were in a relationship with a fire or a water sign, I should consider making a change and search for an earth mate. I had a choice of three: Taurus, Virgo or Capricorn. She advised me that a Capricorn would not be a very good choice. Lisa was not quite done. She was finished with improving my love life and was moving on to my work life stars and the best way to manage my career. Lisa spoke to me until I reached my destination. I finally said four words as I stood to leave: "Thank you. Take care."

My commute was a very interesting 40 minutes long. I surprised myself; I could refrain from speaking for 40 minutes. I was walking home from the subway realizing the amount of knowledge I had just consumed about tarot cards, Indian astrology, Chinese astrology and their animal signs. I now know that sun signs, star signs and zodiac signs are all the same, just share different names.

This wasn't a phobia. It was spiritual strength that made her feel good about herself. It was entertaining for me, but knowledge I will never need. Her interest was remarkable but what was exceptional was her commitment to astrology. She believed that learning more and more about astrology would enhance her well-being.

There was a lesson to be learned: We all have hope, faith and sometimes we need to believe in something besides ourselves.

> "We judge ourselves by what we feel capable of doing, while others judge us by what we have already done."
>
> —Longfellow

Commuting Can Be Amusing

Making a trip to the zoo to observe the animals can amuse our minds, while others relish the idea of visiting aquariums to appreciate existence in the waters. Have you ever observed and appreciated humans?

Visit a New York City subway and derive joy from a simple train ride. You hopefully can locate an empty seat and begin your observation immediately. There is no need for pens, pencils or paper; this is meant for visual appreciation only.

My commute home to and from work is approximately a 40-minute ride on the subway. I observe my surroundings only by reason of boredom. I was in a rush to get home and didn't bring reading material along for the ride. I boarded the train, took a seat and my eyes observed....

The doors opened and a young woman entered the train. This woman had every strand of hair in place; her lipstick showed no wear and her posture was perfect. She made her entrance and noticed a seat across from me. She did not appear a bit fatigued and it was slightly after the evening rush hour. She placed her purse on top of her thighs while seated. Minutes later she was searching inside her purse and found herself a stick of gum. That was when I knew her image was in jeopardy. She began with cracking her gum and later moved on to making small bubbles which she could unattractively suck back into her mouth just to repeat the cracking procedure.

A man dressed for success sat next to me. As I watched the woman across the way making incomparable bubbles, I still couldn't help noticing the man's attire. A sharply dressed man with burnished shoes, he silently placed his briefcase between his legs. A couple of minutes passed and he reached for his briefcase. I was hoping he wasn't going to search for a stick of gum. He placed his briefcase on his lap. He opened it only to reveal his newspaper. The newspaper was the only item in the briefcase. (Must have a stress-free job without overtime hours.) He had a hard time just folding his newspaper. The paper was huge when fully drawn and the passenger next to him would need some personal space. I was watching him go through an overflow of work so he could read a different page. His arms were receiving plenty of exercise.

I think the kid sitting next to the chewing gum queen didn't hear the gum cracking because he was busy singing. I considered it to be singing. In between the lyrics he could make noise like instruments. Talented kid.

Others aboard the train were conversing to one another, sleeping or reading. I was just observing. There was a box in between the legs of a middle-aged woman. A brown box the size of a pet carrier for a cat or small dog. The brown box had string around it with a handle for easy transportation. I heard a scratching noise. It was the box. Other noises that I couldn't figure out were coming from inside the box.

The box tried to relocate to an unknown location on the train. I was the only one who saw the box in motion. Everyone was busy keeping themselves amused and occupied. That oblivious behavior came to an end when the box broke open. There were about 30 people riding on the subway car. The box

MY WORLD: JUMP IN ANYTIME!

revealed eight energetic lobsters and panic swirled within the subway car.

I had no idea why they had claws that were not restricted prior to trapping them inside a cardboard box. The owner of the box was trying to catch them, and her hands were bleeding from the hunt. What would she do if she apprehended them? Where would she put them? She no longer had a box. There were no feet upon the floor of the subway car and I couldn't help the asinine grin upon my face.

The man with his newspaper began to swat the creatures with his annoying noisy uncontrollable newspaper, the woman stopped chewing her gum to make screaming possible and the kid with the earphones put his feet up on the seat and continued singing with a smile. Others were screaming and trying to escape to the next subway car. A vision to witness.

At the next train stop, an adventurous lobster decided to abandon his traveling mates and depart through the open doors. All I could think about was the individual who was to confront that lobster on the subway platform. My stop was next…but I left alone. I walked onto the platform, lobster free, down the stairs and onto the street knowing that would be a lifelong memory and noone should ever commute with lobsters. Lobsters cause chaos.

An Airport Experience

I decided to visit an old friend from years past, which meant a very long commute ahead of me. My friend had been residing in Texas for the past few years, and I had not paid a visit since he moved. I was aware of the four-hour flight but wasn't aware of the volume of travelers.

To travel during any holiday is a mistake. It makes no difference what type of traveling: land, sea or air. I was disillusioned with the reality that Thanksgiving was the "big" holiday trip. I tried to figure out when the college kids would travel home and picked a date with that theory in mind. It was bad enough that I really did not want to fly, but the airlines were giving me good reason to get discouraged.

I was unable to get a flight that was non-stop to Texas. I needed to go from New York to Atlanta and then from Atlanta to Texas. The stop-over was going to take time, but I really wanted to see my friend. I decided to make the trip on December 28. I thought it was a perfect time to travel and all the travelers were where they should be during the holiday. I was wrong. All the travelers were all together in Atlanta.

My anxiety level was off the charts with the concept that I needed to get on a plane surrounded by a gigantic mass of people. The last few years airport security had been extremely thorough and travelers needed to be at the airport almost two hours before their flight. The policy of checking luggage and taking shoes off when walking through security devices would be enough stress, until I heard "Boarding flight...." The reality of stress was now an issue as never before.

I was just waiting around the airport listening to the constant recording over the sound system: "If you see any suspicious individuals, please contact an airline member." The airport was helping me heighten my fears because the recording was heard every 15 minutes. I started thinking that a tranquilizer would be an good option right then. I began to pace, waiting to board the plane until I was mentally and physically exhausted.

I sat down across from someone's carry-on luggage. After a few moments, an airport employee started asking questions loudly to the passengers surrounding her. I recalled some of those questions: "Whose bag is this?" "Does this bag belong to anyone?" Next thing you know, all within minutes, one employee used the walkie-talkie they diligently hold on to and four security members walked toward the bag from all different directions. At that time, five people were surrounding this bag. At that time, I found the water cooler and made the tranquilizer a must for my body. From the corner of my eye I could see a woman in her twenties walking in the direction of the bag holding a soft drink. All I could think was how fortunate I was not to be her. All eyes were fixed upon her and security asked, "Ma'am, is this your bag?"

The woman wished it wasn't her bag but announced, "Yeah, it's mine."

The reprimanding began and I heard, "Ma'am, under no circumstance, are you ever to leave a bag unattended." It went on and on. Each in the huddle had something to add to the reprimanding process.

I know it doesn't state upon the walls of the airport to never leave luggage unattended, but we live in a different world than in the years past. Years ago you would worry that someone could take your luggage; today we worry someone will leave luggage behind purposely.

Soon after the commotion ended, I heard, "Boarding flight…"

I was then sitting on the plane, just thinking to myself. When others asked, "So, how was your flight?" I'd give the standard answer: "Okay."

When people asked, "How are you?" they aren't waiting for an extensive answer, they are just being polite.

> "Love doesn't make the world go around. Love is what makes the ride worthwhile."
>
> —Franklin P. Jones

Fish in the Sea

My grandmother was a young girl when she lost family members aboard the "unsinkable ship." The *Titanic* sank in 1912. The ship collided into an iceberg and in just two and a half hours the vessel broke in two and sank to over 1,200 feet below the water's surface. The ship lies on the bottom of the North Atlantic Ocean. The sinking of that ship was only the beginning of heartache for that generation.

The population that was born in the early 1900s had their share of pain and struggling through the times. Success was measured by the mere fact of bringing forth food on the table for your family. Susie, my grandmother, was the woman who could have given me an earful when she was alive. She, as well as others of her generation, lived through World War I, Pearl Harbor, World War II, the Great Depression, the Korean War and the Vietnam War. Born at a time when the Wright brothers were destined to fly and Henry Ford introduced automobiles. In the 1920s, the 19th amendment gave the right of voting to women.

My generation could have acquired knowledge through conversations from the eyes of those who had survived through what we only have literature as our teacher. I never took advantage of the opportunity to ask my female forebear any questions about her past. The prospect of education through experience is now lost.

I recall entering her home and she would be making her famous raisin rice pudding. Lawrence Welk was in view on the television set, and I would wind each of her musical figurines that sat upon her wooden dresser. I would watch the cuckoo clock every hour for childish excitement. (Behavior I still haven't outgrown.)

It is so many years later. I spent time with her through the years but few memories stay clear in my mind. If I continue to reminisce the memories I own, they will stay apparent as I grow old. All those years ago I had a minute interest in my grandmother's past. Today, so many questions will go unanswered for my missed opportunities. There is one thing I will always remember. It took me a remarkably long time to comprehend her concept. I have it down to a science and I am the authority on her life-long lesson: fishing.

She never owned a fishing pole. No need for one. *Fish* was a term for *men*. I had a history of catching poor fish. Not really "poor" fish, just fish that caught my bait accidentally. "If this fish isn't big enough—throw him back. Better fish in the sea."—a statement she would pronounce with confidence and authority. It sounded like a gamble to me. If I threw a fish back, how did I know the next catch would be an improvement? My logic: keep the fish and keep fishing. When I found one I wanted to detain, I'd discard the other fish to the sea for others to hook. The words still could be heard: "Throw it back. You'll know when the right fish is on the hook!"

I should have listened and read between the lines. My grandmother had found her perfect fish many years ago. The fish moved to its final destination before I was born. She never went fishing again. For over 30 years, she swam solo. My grandmother never wanted another knowing she had already found the best in the sea. She taught my father to fish. My father was a great fisherman. He caught my mom. Yes, an outstanding fisherman.

    A gamble worth taking, I threw all the fish back in the sea. I observed the water. With eyes wide open, I reeled in the best. My grandmother had departed to encounter her exquisite fish once again, in her final destination. I am now prepared to give lessons and lectures about fishing. (It has taken me decades to grasp the concept.) Meanwhile, my grandmother enjoyed working when she was existing on earth and I am sure that she is, in her final destination, teaching. Chances are she is teaching Fishing 101, 102 and so on.

    There are many fish in the sea.

    Fish to find the ultimate fish.

    Never settle.

    I get it now.

    (Some of us may need to hang up the pole and just jump in the water.)

> "Do not take life too seriously. You will never get out of it alive."
>
> —Hubbard

Dreams, Nightmares or Daydreams

Believe in your dreams. My thought on this statement is positively negative. Have you ever uncovered a dream book, dictionary or handbook? I have. My curiosity led me to a local bookshop in lower Manhattan. This shop had many books on the subject. I am sure those books were big sellers in that particular neighborhood. Surrounding the bookshop, you can visit psychics, fortunetellers, palm readers and astrology advisors that are ready to assist you. I did buy a dream book for entertaining purposes only. It was dispiriting.

First I need to explain that I know the important facts on sleep and dreaming. Simple facts. No analyzing. Concrete evidence according to medical technology. The electroencephalograph (EEG) measures our brain's electrical activity. We begin with alpha waves and work through four different stages of sleep; the fourth stage is considered delta waves. Then we reach REM sleep and dreaming occurs at this final stage. The brain's activity is at the strongest during REM sleep. This is healthy for the mind and body. I have read that the average American person gets approximately six hours of sleep per day. We all dream in color but have no fixed meaning.

This is all I needed to know about sleep and dreams. I thought I had this area all covered.

I was wrong.

Analyzing dreams is oppressive, overwhelming and exhausting. When I was in the bookshop, I compared different dream books and the meanings were identical. Dream descriptions are universal and a diminutive possibility of different views or definitions. These definitions are written laws on interpreting dreams.

I have read Sigmund Freud's view on dreams from various studies that he conducted. He was a medical doctor who specialized in neurology and worked with psychiatric patients. He developed his theory through research on patients. Our mind is filled with unconscious thoughts rather than conscious thoughts. He believed that we dream to fulfill our wishes. Most of his theories related to sex and aggression. All our repressed passions are released during our sleep stages. It is possible to dream of something related to the day prior because of the subconscious mind, whether it is a place, a person or an object.

Skimming through dream books I found that some believe we can solve our problems by interpreting the meanings of our dreams. Some even still believe that dreams are messages from the gods. Medical books claim that women dream longer than men and both sexes need to sleep on the right-hand side for better sleep while your bed is in a north-south position. Plenty of hours of research.

I am apprehensive to wallow away into dreamland. It is frightening. I could dream about teeth. That is a horrendous omen. Nothing good will come of teeth. Obtain a dictionary of dreams and investigate teeth. You will uncover words such as suffering, afraid, unhappiness and losing—all in one definition. I imagine if I dream of the tooth fairy, I may have to anticipate death.

Fish. (Did I mention my appreciation for fish?) Fish are gladly received in a dream. This is extraordinary. I searched and found the definition of fish in my dream dictionary. In the description, I read powerful and positive words: sex, money, power, indulge and love. I thought this was great until I continued reading. Fish, as a general category, is great. Don't dream of sharks and oysters. Very unfortunate. If you dream of eels, sardines, crabs, anchovies, jellyfish, scallops or lobsters you are in some type of dilemma. The best advice I would give—forget you dreamt about any particular fish. Be safe, put your mind at ease and look up general fish.

I do not want to start my morning with coffee in one hand and a dream book in another. I do not need to know my future misfortunes. I am never well prepared. If I dream my spouse is cheating, it would mean an illness is approaching my way or a financial bind will strike me. I don't feel the need to know in advance. No need to worry about such happenings. Most people I have met spend more time worrying about things that never happen.

Maybe I should explore a Native American shop. The ancient world of the Ojibwe nation was the home of spiritual clans located in a place known as Turtle Island. These are the spiritual people who designed dream catchers. No work involved. No big philosophical explanations. The dream catcher filters out all bad *bawedjigewin* (dreams) and only good dreams are to come through and enter our minds. All I need to do is hang it up over my bed. Little work for me and I will have peace of mind. No fear of dreaming. Very attractive to the eye. Appears to be a small hula-hoop, with spider webs entwined and then a big feather lies in the center. The feather represents breath or air. An owl's feather is mostly for women; it is the wisdom feather. The eagle's feather is for courage and is

predominately for the male. I am confident in this investment. Simple, decorative and no stress involved.
    I have abandoned my dream dictionary. No longer will I make the usual request of "sweet dreams." That sweet dream you encounter may not be so sweet. When I dream, I want it to be displeasing and unfavorable. When I wake in the morning hours, I am so relieved that it all was only a dream. Simple.
    Take control.
    Dream worry free.
    Believe in your daydreams.

> "The proper office of a friend is to side with you when you are wrong. Nearly anybody will side with you when you are right."
>
> —Mark Twain

Children at Play

Occasionally my ears absorb the noise that surrounds me. Most of the time I am too preoccupied with my thoughts to take notice of any other sounds besides my personal thoughts. Now and then I stop to appreciate my environment.

I decided to pay close attention to those around me at a nearby park. It was brunch time when I decided to visit the playground. I love to speak with my elders and the park is a fine place for easy conversation. I love to listen to their past experiences. They find enjoyment when I show interest and this makes me feel good about myself. I need to be attentive and my elders appreciate me.

At one point I believed the old saying: "Things were different when I was a kid." I have heard these words many times before from generations prior to mine. As time passed I believed the same was true. Was I brain washed from all those around me? Then again, have we changed, as we grew older?

Youth is so terrific. Five great reasons: No need to worry about finances. Racism does not exist. You never know that you are tired. Weather never has any affect on you. You suppose that nothing ever comes to an end.

I noticed one group of creative children playing musical chairs. They were very creative since they didn't have chairs at the park but they had chalk.

The game of musical chairs has one less child than chairs. Each time the music is played, the children circle around the chairs. The music comes to a halt and the children scurry and scramble around for a chair to sit on. The child left standing is out and so is one chair. This is continued until one chair is left with the winner sitting upon the chair.

These young children had drawn boxes on the floor. When the music stopped, you needed to find a box to stand on rather than a chair to sit upon. What was even more amusing was their music predicament. They had none. One very smart girl decided she would sing and when she stopped singing they needed to find a box that they had handmade upon concrete. Instead of taking away a chair, they simply scribbled over a box. The very smart girl was the winner each game—wasn't so tough since she was in control over the music playing. One very smart boy caught on. He decided he should sing the music for the next game. She insisted that she was the best among their voices. He claimed that she was a cheater and he began to walk away from her and the others. Shouts could be heard from the circle of children. You could hear them taunting the small boy: "Flat leaver!"

He was unaffected by their name-calling. He continued to walk toward another circle of children. He was confident, not easily intimated and the only child to recognize that girl was cheating. He may become a very successful CEO. I couldn't help but consider their futures. That very smart girl was not only sly but had the ability to sway the others to follow her motives. She'd probably be a political figure or the president of an activist group…she had what it takes.

As the elders in the park continued to watch and smile at the children playing, you could see they were smiling upon youth.

Maybe, just maybe, they were thinking: *Things haven't drastically changed.*

    I conclude that youth is laborious. A game of musical chairs is considered to be fun. "Simple" games can become "difficult" to play at any age. Life is a game: You never know how long you will play. At times you are a step ahead and other times a step behind. Its outcome is not predictable.

    Keep in mind that you will never know how long you'll play the game.

    Have fun.

    Just play.

Bond between brothers,
They have independent thoughts,
A dependent love.

—Susan Thomas Alexandria

Unconditional Love

Two brothers wait for a snowstorm. So many positive reasons for snow to fall in any child's opinion. School will be canceled, sled riding, making a snowman, having snowball fights, making snow angels and then grabbing a shovel and making money. The old saying goes: Be careful of what you wish for...because it just may come true. (I believe that old saying.) It snowed. The snow fell about 30 inches deep one winter day.

Two brothers, an eleven- and thirteen-year-old, leave their home searching to find work and make some money. No sooner do the boys leave their home than an elderly couple notices the boys holding their shovels. The couple lives a few houses away and they need help with the mounds of snow covering their property. The woman offers the boys forty dollars to clear the snow. The area to be cleared is quite large, but so is the sum of money offered to them.

It is work. Hard work. After an hour of shoveling in the cold, the older brother explains that he needs to use the bathroom, get a drink and change his gloves. The younger brother keeps working. He already has the money spent that he hasn't finished earning. He doesn't stop. Almost an hour later the young brother finishes the job...alone.

He rings the bell of the couple, very wearily claims that he has finished clearing the snow. The woman hands him his forty well-earned dollars and he thanks her repeatedly. His body is tired and he just wants to go home.

The young boy enters his home only to find his big brother watching television and drinking hot chocolate. He has cleaned himself and changed into his warm comfortable sweatsuit with big warm socks. The younger brother walks to him without uttering a word and tosses him twenty dollars and he turns to leave the room to take off his cold, wet clothes. Negotiations had never taken place.

I am dumbfounded. I raised those two boys the same and the result was two different kids. The young eleven-year-old boy continues to admire his thirteen-year-old sibling. I am the bureaucrat of our family. Every parent is a lawmaker. I make inflexible rules. I play fair. I take ten dollars from the older one and give it back to the younger son. Fair. The older should get ten dollars and the younger deserves the thirty dollars.

Here comes the puzzling part of the mini family dilemma: Neither looks happy that I corrected their income. My oldest son is angry that I interfered in the deal-making process and the younger one is still coming to the oldest child's defense stating that it was his idea to shovel in the first place. If anyone person other than his brother performed a disappearing act while shoveling, the outcome wouldn't be fifty-fifty. Trust me.

Like I said: "I am an only child missing a bond."

These two brothers define: *Blood is thick and much thicker than water.*

> And now these three remain: faith, hope and love. But the greatest of these is love.
>
> —1 Corinthians 13:13

Wedding Bands

I thought purchasing wedding bands was relatively effortless. There was a colleague of mine, Maria, who unknowingly wanted to prove me wrong. (Little did she know that this was the easy part of marriage.) This subject of bands was the topic of conversation that lasted for many weeks within our company. I was not the only coworker subjected to her dilemma. Some other coworkers gave their view: "Go for the most expensive." Others would comment: "Your wedding band must match your engagement ring." After all the hours of work involved in her decision making I could only hope that her marriage would last her whole life long. (Till death.)

Maria, three other colleagues and myself were standing by the water cooler. A perfect place for quick conversation. If Maria decided to open her mouth the only words to flow out would be about her wedding band decisions. I wondered if we needed to be subjected to her decisions in any other wedding areas: photos, flowers and favors. Just before any words could escape her mouth, a male coworker turned to Maria: "Who cares? Does he care? Will he even wear one?" Maria's facial expression revealed her disgust and hatred for him as she briskly walked away from all of us. For the remainder of the day she was quiet and kept her distance from everyone in the office. She probably was able to get some work done for a change of pace. Recently her time was spent on deliberations for her personal dilemmas. Was my male coworker brave enough to conclude the conversation ever continuing with Maria? No.

Tomorrow was yet another day. I was her first victim. She walked over to my desk holding a catalog of rings. I got it. She wanted feedback. Not one of us in the office looked remotely interested nor did we give concrete criticism. We had the same neutral response: "Oh, nice."

I decided to give my opinion and participate in the wedding decisions, praying this would be the very last wedding she would ever have to organize. My family and friends often tell me that I store so much useless information in my brain that I will never use or need. The useless information on wedding rings that I stored in memory, I needed to share with Maria.

We decided to have lunch together the following day and agreed the weather was so perfect we could just grab a slice of pizza and take a stroll in Central Park. Maria is young and I knew this because she made it a point to tell me she hadn't reached the legal drinking age in New York, and if she drank alcohol at the wedding it would be a crime. She was still young enough to be the sponge seeking others to absorb knowledge. That was where I came in. I was going to educate her and give a private lesson on the history of the wedding band and what it means to us today.

While taking our stroll through the park, I said to Maria: "I want to share with you what I know about wedding rings." She eagerly awaited my story just because I was the only person to seem remotely interested in wedding bands. The history goes back centuries and I begin my input:

"Many men did not wear wedding bands prior to the 1930s. The wedding band became popular during wartime. It was a constant reminder of their wives at home. For spiritual or philosophical reasons it became popular for men to wear their band of gold.

"I have read that the Egyptians are responsible for the ring ceremony over 4,000 years ago. They made exchanges with rings made of hemp and reedy plants. They made it into a string-like material by rolling it through their fingers. Men and women were treated as one. Equal. Both parties for their spiritual love wore rings.

"It is difficult to say the origin of the ring but many have the idea that the first rings were made of grass, bone and base metals. Iron was used by the Romans, but only for the women to wear to show ownership to a man. Men were never to be 'owned' by any one woman.

"Tradition declares that the ring needs to be placed on the fourth finger of the left hand for eternal love. This finger contains the love vein that runs straight to the heart. The Romans called this vein: Vena Amoris.

"The Greeks introduced devotion rings that were worn as a symbol of loyalty and commitment. The Greeks have always worn their wedding rings on the fourth finger of the right hand just the same as all the Orthodox Christians today.

"Jewish ceremonies exchange rings and place them on the right index finger. The right index finger is the finger of intelligence. When the ceremony ends, the bride places the ring on the fourth finger of her right hand.

"Many years ago the Colonial Americans felt that wedding rings did not serve a useful purpose. Instead of rings they exchanged thimbles as their token for their marriage. Soon after the women would cut the bottom of the thimble to make their own wedding bands.

"Poesy rings are my personal favorite. Poesy can be spelled p-o-s-e-y or p-o-s-y. Shakespeare would refer to the poesy rings in many of his plays and the ring was very popular during the 16th and 17th centuries.

"The poesy ring was given to a woman in silver or white gold as a betrothal ring. When the marriage took place the rings during the ceremony would be given in gold to replace the silver or white ring. Both bands could be worn together. Two words were inscribed anywhere on the ring: **Love and hope.**"

Maria just listened to all I had to say about the history of wedding ring bonds and I thought it was clear it was a symbol. I knew about her taste in jewelry, but I didn't even know the name of her husband to be.

The next working day she walked over to another co-worker and I heard: "So do you like this one or this one better?" I guess I wasted my breath as well as my knowledge in the materialistic society we have created. Doesn't the importance lie within the aspect or the meaning it holds? Measure not the size of the diamond but measure the size of the man's heart.

Later that day I went into a local store and made a purchase. I can't remember the purchase but I remember the cashier. The cashier who assisted me had a plain band of gold around her finger.

I thought to myself: *She gets it.* Love and Hope.

The ring is not important. The man who gives it is.

"Finish each day and be done with it. You have done what you could; some blunders and absurdities have crept in; forget them as soon as you can. Tomorrow is a new day; you shall begin it serenely and with too high a spirit to be encumbered with your old nonsense."

—Ralph Waldo Emerson

Technology

I put forth effort to keep up with technology and I consider it a job. It shares similarities associated with a job: stress and knowledge. In a couple of decades our society has made major breakthroughs in our technological world.

The first VCR was four times the size of the VCR systems of today. Almost every home today owns at least one computer. In only two decades we were introduced to home video games, personal computers, digital cameras, cellular phones, compact discs and DVDs.

My neighbor has a sixteen-year-old daughter, Aimee, who often stops in my house for a visit. I have watched her grow from a small toddler into a beautiful young lady. One of her visits will always prevail in my memory.

Aimee walked into my home during a big cleaning day. Closet day requires the entire day. Not because I have huge closets, but the amount I store in small closets becomes a job for the day. I retain shoeboxes filled with "stuff." Instead of stacking all the boxes together, I begin to fumble through each of these boxes. I study the contents: read the cards, look through the notes and examine each ticket stub I have saved from some concert, show or movie I once attended. Forty minutes had passed and I still had a dozen more shoe boxes to

explore. I decided to move to another part of the closet. (That was when Aimee came in.) I was looking through the music section of my closet.
Albums or LPs and records known as 45s. I have a large collection of music. I have a storage spindle for the 45s I have collected through the years and I still feel the need to breeze through each of these records. I fumble through piles of records and read each and every title. Actually, I find myself singing each title to the beat of the song. I uncover a song I would like to hear while taking on the closet chore. I take the 45-speed record in my hand, place it on the record player and place the needle upon the vinyl circle. From that moment it was an unfamiliar sound to her ears. She had never heard the sound of the needle on vinyl seconds before the music began. She did not say a word until the song ended. Aimee then spoke: "You got robbed. One song from that big disc."
What did she know at sixteen years old? Compact disc were all she had experienced with the fifteen songs with eighty minutes of music on each disc. After she told me that I was robbed because only one song was on my 45, she went on to question: "So, that is like an antique?" I never thought of my memories as antiques! While Aimee questioned me she was on her cell phone just about to email her friend. Technology.
I have memories of my girlfriends and I sitting around playing music and chatting about everything teenage girls enjoy. The record player was a big deal when I was a kid. (Not so long ago.)
I didn't dare withdraw the typewriter or my 8-track player from the closet as long as Aimee was still in my presence. How could I explain the ancient technology to one who already believes that my closet contains only antiques?

Soldier

Freedom. Independence. Liberty. Three words the majority of us take for granted. When faced with evil and tragedy we then remind ourselves of those three words. Our parents and the generations prior have served our country and given us the pride we share today.

In the distance, a soldier stands,
Knowing his fate is in God's hands.
He has given his all, done his part,
The soldier will live forever in America's heart.

Inhaling the air
Unfamiliar surroundings
Unpredictable

Containing their fears
In God's hands, their fate is held
Together they pray

Far distance from home
Determination for peace
Quest for one's freedom

SUSAN T.A. SAKELOS

To fear the unknown
They stand committed to each
They would be as one

Their sacrifices,
Every soldier lives in our hearts
America's pride.

> "Fame is the perfume of heroic deeds."
>
> —Socrates

Fame

"In the future, everybody will have 15 minutes of fame."
—Andy Warhol

    I wholeheartedly agree with the famous artist, one of the leaders in the Pop Art movement in the 1960s. You will agree with his statement if you put that statement in perspective. Initially you need to consider how you measure success. You need to make yourself familiar with the definition of fame. Public esteem.

    Fame has no limits or rules. Fame can be acquired in a classroom of 20 students or from television with millions of viewers. Fame does not require the invention of a new vaccine or a cure for a deadly disease. Fame is measured by an individual's emotions and self-satisfaction.

    Fame can be felt from the home run hit to win the baseball game, a basketball shot to win just as the buzzer sounds, the small payoff from the long-awaited win from the casino slot machine, the school spelling bee or a career promotion.

    As for myself, I know I have captured many 15-minute segments in my years. My feeling of "fame" was experienced when I reached the age of six. Fame to a six-year-old is simple.

    You are encircled by a considerable amount of children

approximately your own age. All of the children are standing next to you in front of the nickel toy machine. All eyes are investigating the contents in the machine. (Not so long ago they were the nickel and dime machines. Now they accept only quarters. Don't fear because many casinos will accept dimes and nickels. Then again they accept all donations. I felt the need to clarify since half of the population probably never heard of the five and dime store.) All the children desire the same toy in that machine. You place your change in the slot of the machine, taking in air with a deep breath and with much anticipation you turn the knob. You exhale. You hear the toy drop down and you open the flap. Just what you hoped for descends into the palm of your hand. Try to remember (not only in your youth), how many times you have glanced up to the sky and whispered: "If you do this for me, I will never ask for anything again."

Fame can be accomplished at any stage in life. Fame is a proud feeling you receive from others or perhaps feedback from that life that you have inspired. Someone can make you feel irreplaceable and that is fame as well. Fame can be general and not so specific.

Within 15 minutes: My four sons are strolling alongside of me on the Atlantic City boardwalk. We have conversations about anything and everything. We play kick-the-can on the boardwalk and our elders know the game and pass us wearing smiles. We all admire the sunset along the horizon. There were five of us gazing upon the ocean but now there are four. The one child that went astray from his family is just across the way; he is bending down to place a dollar bill into a musician's collection cup. As he strolls back to the family, he just smiles at me. I never utter a word, I just throw my arms around him and gave him a big squeeze. A huge embrace to be remembered.

MY WORLD: JUMP IN ANYTIME!

We start walking along the boardwalk to indulge in some ice cream; we have conversation and inhale the scent of the ocean. When the ocean's gentle breeze arrives we can taste the salt upon our lips. We are scattered around our small family circle with few people around us. My two younger sons are chasing the seagulls and I am enjoying their display of energy. Suddenly I hear in a strong, sincere voice: "God bless you, son." I was so preoccupied enjoying my family that I did not notice the man who was only feet away from where I stood until he spoke. The man's legs had been amputated and he was wheelchair bound. He was begging for money as many others do along the boardwalk. I did not observe whom the man was addressing until I noticed Vince standing close by the man. Vincent was a few feet ahead of me strolling in the opposite direction from the family. I hustled to catch up to him. He gave the handicapped man money with no knowledge that his brother gave money to an unemployed musician on the opposite side of the boardwalk. I questioned my first born: "Vincent, was that man in the wheelchair speaking to you?" My son, with glassy eyes and a lump in his throat, just nodded.

I have little men with big hearts. They fortunately possess the gift of compassion.

A display of humanity.

Many things can transpire in 15 minutes.

This fame will last me a lifetime.

What is fame to the famous? Famous people must have a different definition than the non-famous people when the topic is fame. I define famous as the one who is in the public eye.

Living in New York I have met quite a few famous people. I never asked them about their own personal 15 minutes. I assume it would be the ability to stroll on an avenue in New York for 15 minutes uninterrupted.

I was working in the fifties on Broadway and *George* magazine was located in the same building. John F. Kennedy Jr. was the founder of that political magazine. I watched him get off his bicycle, walk into the lobby and enter the elevator without any hassle, just smiles and the common good morning. That must have been a great five minutes instead of fifteen.

A friend of mine, Nick, who just so happened to employ me for many years, introduced me to his world. He had very popular, famous and prestigious friends. Among them were writers from popular New York newspapers, magazines, books; some were business owners, another individual was a radio talk show host and one was a musical entertainer as well as a writer. His name: Kinky Friedman. All of Nick's friends were enjoyable but Kinky stood out in a crowd, not just for his accomplishments but for his mannerisms.

One evening I joined approximately a dozen of Nick's friends for dinner with Kinky among the dozen. When I stood from our large round table to visit the ladies room, he stood up as well. When I returned he quickly stood up and pulled my chair out for me. The second we both were seated again, he has a light ready for the woman on his opposite side with a cigarette in hand. He was busy that evening just because of his kindness and I couldn't help but wonder if all Southern men were gentlemen. He was a great guy with a sense of humor because he knew I kept getting up out of my chair to test his patience and character. Each time I stood, he stood. The first time he stood up I remember asking: "Where are you going?" He just grinned and sat down. He passed the test with flying colors. He was one of the finest gentlemen I have ever encountered. So when asked how my evening was at the finest steak house in New York, I could only answer: "I was in the company of a gentleman that evening."

MY WORLD: JUMP IN ANYTIME!

That is an example of an emotion of fame.

A warm, breezy day in June, I left work early and decided to bring my work home with me. It was late afternoon when I was waiting for an express bus on East 14th Street and Broadway. I started fumbling through my work wanting to acquire an article I was planning on reading once I was in the bus. Not to my surprise, I dropped all my papers and the breeze was ready to swirl down Broadway. I remember I wore a blue and ivory skirt, my hair was braided and it was three o'clock in the afternoon on June 18, 1991. I remember all of this day. This day I met a man who many knew on the silver screen.

I started to collect my papers off the sidewalk; I turned my head toward the street and watched my bus pass me by. I turned back to continue picking up my papers and a man helped me gather them together. We stood up at the same time and he looked so familiar. He was wearing camouflage clothing and he had very little hair, looked like he was on leave from the service. I asked him, "Do you work in the Lincoln Plaza corporate building?"

He answered, "No." He said nothing and I guessed a few more places that I may have met him. He told me that he was heading downtown and asked if I was heading in the same direction. I decided to walk a few blocks until the next bus stop.

After a couple of blocks I asked, "All right. I can't place you. What do you do for a living?"

He answered with a grin, "I'm an actor."

We were walking around in the village where all the struggling actors work as waiters. I responded, "So—you're a waiter."

He smiled and kept walking and I heard him say, "I am visiting, I don't live here."

We went into a bookstore and I glanced around the store

and from the corner of my eye, he was heading to the lower level. I remained on the street level and waited for him to return. At first he didn't see me and then he said to me, "I thought you left."

I recall saying, "I would have said goodbye to you first."

We stopped outside another store to do some window shopping until the moment a few young women noticed him. Fame. I was walking with Keanu Reeves.

We were waiting for the light to change on Houston Street and there was a movie theater on the corner. The theater was showing, A Midsummer Night's Dream. I looked at the billboard, then at him and said, "Look. It's you."

I remember us talking about Canada, his family and his band, Dog Star. It was easy conversation. I wish he wasn't "famous" and I think he knew that thought, which he entertained. My fame was simple: I was so ecstatic that he was in my company and not so much that I had met a superstar. He was such a pleasant person and it was so easy to be in his company. I believe his fame was the mere fact I treated him like any non-famous individual on the streets of New York.

It was getting late into the evening and we parted with, "Take care. So nice to meet you."

We all measure fame on different levels and values.

> "Love at home is the foundation for peace in the world."
>
> —Mother Teresa

Lightning Bug Fun

Objective: Let children…be children. (Let adults…be children.) Time is the greatest gift you can give to a child. Quality time. It is accomplished by sharing your childhood activities with your own children. Generation to generation. The cycle of life.

My claimed childish behavior is confirmed each time, without exception, when I pay a visit to my sons' rooms or to our family playroom. I enter my oldest son's room and he is conquering the latest computer game. It appears to be a challenging game. Excitedly, I tell my son Vincent, "Wow, I got next." Knowing that I play next because I called it, I visit another room occupied by another son of mine. This son has a collection of wind-up toys. I always seem to wind up one of those toys for no reason but to see it in motion. My son Thomas is busy putting a model plane together and he is so focused on his project that we have no conversation. I go and return to the previous room to find the oldest still playing the computer game and I am impatient to try this game and he is so engrossed with his eyes upon the screen, that I decide to give up and play another time. I terminate my visit with both the boys and go down a flight of stairs to the playroom and find my youngest sons playing with their toys. They too are paying little attention to me. I am annoyed that my four sons ignore me as if I was a child seeking attention.

Now I act like the adult of our home. I start picking up toys left on the floor of the playroom and return them to the toy box when I notice the magic black ball. This magic ball must have called me by name because I find myself walking toward the ball on the shelf. The manufacturer has made this ball for many decades. In that time (I am convincing myself), I am not alone with the compelling feeling to play this foolish game. I pick it up and ask this ball a question (out loud no less). I shake the ball gently and turn it upside down to reveal the answer to my question.

Here is this ball that contains a triangle floating in fluid and when you turn it upside down the triangle just floats to the top and randomly turns to reveal an answer. Answers are limited: "yes," "no," "maybe," "ask later" and "try again."

As if it wasn't childish enough to ask a question in the first place, I am now unhappy with the answer I received. Now I begin to think I should try again and I hear myself say, "Okay, two out of three." I am playing with a magic ball for entertaining purposes only. I am entertained for a short time until I become frustrated with the ball and once again I hear myself say, "Okay, three out of five."

I manage to put my childish behavior to good use. I tell my four boys that I am a great hunter and this evening we will share some family time together on a hunting expedition. My sons are just staring at me and I excitedly say, "Tonight we hunt. No lightning bug will be safe in our town this evening." Thomas breaks the silence: "I'm ready."

After supper all the boys prepare to leave the house and begin the hunt. The sport of catching fireflies is limited to a short hunting season. July in New York is the best time to capture these beetles. We are prepared and our equipment includes all we need to get the job done successfully...nets, jars and jugs. (I can always count on at least one son wearing camouflage for the entire hunting effect.)

We walk out the door, descend down the stairs and head to the firefly grounds. Tommy exclaims, "Hope we don't capture the poisonous flying beetles." He brings adventures in a new light. Tommy reads obscure material that I usually don't examine too closely. It isn't unusual for him to learn information and retain what he has learned, but I never ask how he has acquired his knowledge. He will recall the facts but has no idea where he found the information. Tommy has his standard answer: "I read it somewhere." My standard reply: "Can't believe everything you read."

I know that the family is in for a very informative evening. Not only will the evening be educational but also a competition will take place. A boy's voice from a competitive family speaks: "The first to catch a dozen lightning bugs will be the winner." No reward for winning except the title of "Champion," which is good enough for these boys. Everyone is ready and I begin: "Ready. Set. Go."

The competition begins and all that is heard repeatedly from all four boys: "I got one." Each boy will believe he is the winner and I can't recall who was the real winner, I only remember the lessons learned through our experiences together.

Cole is so proud of his new "friends" he captured and he continues to stare and examine his bugs. While staring inside his jug he inquires, "Can I keep them?" I am about to answer him when Tommy interrupts and decides to take the matter into his own hands: "They will only live a few days. Very few will even last a month." I know this is a fact and Tommy knows because he probably read it somewhere. These flying beetles only live for a week to a month and this is the time span for their adulthood. They live as flightless larvae for about a year or two then a brief period called pupal stage and then they are considered adults.

The glowing light is a chemical reaction and is used as a mating signal. So I figure that we are interfering with their reproduction cycle. They don't have all that long to mate and lay eggs so we need to free these captured beetles. Cole does not need to be exposed to all this information. So before Tommy gives Cole any details, I quickly state, "We should set them free because we don't want to take him away from his family and friends." A simply response that refers to unity and is easy for a child to understand. Cole admires his lightning bugs and then his little hands open the lid of his jar to set them free. He excitedly screams, "Go and be free, find your brothers!" (I love the idea that Cole thinks everyone—including insects—must have brothers. He does ask everyone he meets, "Where are your brothers?") All my sons let their bugs fly free to light up the sky.

I don't know what amazes me more about these lightning bugs; their instinct, the warm glow of nature or their mission to be accomplished. These beetles may only live for five days and each day counts. Each given day is precious time. If every human being could live each day as if it were the last and never take time for granted, we would live in a very different world.

You can speak of the past and dream of the future, but...Today is the present.

Today is a present.

Appreciate every given day.

Beneath me, the sand
Toward the ocean I stand
A feeling of peace

Perfect Harmony
Strong waves play a symphony
An appreciation

Moonlight will reflect
In the distance, the warm light
My spirit feels free

Contrasting darkness
One bright gleaming star, I stare
Feel the star in reach

Powerful lightning
Mystery that surrounds it
Just as love itself

A light gentle breeze
From the ocean's horizon
Salt upon my lips

When least expected
The breeze takes me by surprise
The way love finds all

Both love and nature
Impressions everlasting
A heart's contentment.

—Susan Thomas Alexandria

> "A faint, cold fear runs through my veins, that almost freezes up the heat of life."
>
> —Shakespeare's Juliet

The Power of Love

Love. So many different views and definitions could be given. What is love? I have a friend who loves seafood, music, steak, her cat and every boyfriend she has encountered in her life. How do we differentiate? How do I differentiate my love for water and all associated; the ocean, lighthouses, and bubble baths? My love for another person? Love is ___?

I was attending a psychology course and one of the requirements had been to conduct a survey. As no surprise to those who knew me during this time, I decided to question love. I randomly chose 80 students from different backgrounds, and a wide range of age groups were included. I instructed these 80 students to write down a word or two defining love on a small white sheet of paper that I handed to them. Everyone followed instructions and folded the paper and placed it into a shoebox that I brought in to school.

Later that day, I took home the shoebox to reveal the responses my fellow students had given to me. After opening the folded sheets of paper, the majority gave standard definitions: Admiration. Fondness. Exciting. Desire. Passion. Others gave me the opposite: Heartache. Stress. One person even wrote: Hate. (Guess that person experienced the fine line between love and hate.)

Love can be misrepresented in old literature. The classic literature emphasizes the bitter end. When you examine the writing of Samson and Delilah or Romeo and Juliet, all you remember are the obstacles and unhappiness that surrounded the characters. The old saying: "Laughing turns to crying" must have been derived by classic literature or even prior to this literature was the reading of mythology.

Before Shakespeare's Romeo and Juliet there was Greek mythology's Pyramus and Thisbe. In Shakespeare's *Midsummer Night's Dream* he referenced the mythical couple, Pyramus and Thisbe. The young beautiful couple had all the odds against their unity. The young lovers lived next door to each other with their parents. They were forbidden to see one another, but a crack in the wall between their homes let them communicate. They would press their opposing lips against the grim wall. Finally they both agreed that they would meet when all was still during late evening hours.

Unhesitating, an agreement made for that evening. They were to meet by the tomb of Ninus. The first to arrive was to await their lover under a distinctive tree outside the tomb. The exquisite tree was a white mulberry tree. Thisbe and Pyramus had impatiently waited for the sun to set and the stars to arrive.

Darkness finally arrived and Thisbe placed a veil over her head and began her quest for her lover's embrace. She was first to arrive at the tomb and waited under the white mulberry tree as agreed. Minutes later Thisbe was startled by a lion that was approaching the stream that was located next to the tree. The lion wore the blood of its latest and most recent kill. Thisbe was terrified and escaped from danger by hiding in a nearby safe place. When she ran for safety, the veil she wore had fallen to the ground. The lion was an enormous curious cat that noticed an unfamiliar sight. He picked up the veil with its bloody mouth and examined the mysterious cloth then just dismissed it to the ground. Thisbe continued to hide in fear when Pyramus reached their ill-fated meeting location. Pyramus was overdue and persistently searched about for Thisbe. In his view was her blood-stained veil. He observed the lion's footprints that left an imprint around her veil. He picked up her veil and began to weep uncontrollably. He knew the veil to be hers and believed that was all that remained of Thisbe.

Pyramus took responsibility for her death. He assumed she had died because he was tardy and unable to protect her from harm. He wearily carried the veil under the tree where he decided his blood should spill on the veil as well as hers. He held her veil in one hand and the other hand held his sword. His tears still flowing upon his cheeks, he thrust his sword through his own heart. His blood splattered all over his surroundings including the white mulberry tree. His blood spilled upon the ground, sinking through the dirt and sand that allowed the tree's roots to absorb his blood.

Thisbe ran toward their meeting place when she doubted her sense of direction. The scenery was not quite the same since the white mulberry tree was no longer white. She worried that she had lost the way to her lover's embrace. She slowly glared around until she looked near the stream located next to the tree and she noticed Pyramus.

Thisbe bent down to embrace his lifeless body with her salty tears falling upon his deadly wounds. He opened his eyes and closed them without a word and she realized that his own hand took his life. Her veil remained in one of his hands as the other still held his sword. She was brave and her love for him was strong as his is for her. Without hesitation, she grabbed his sword and ended her life just as Pyramus had ended his life.

They were forever together, buried in one tomb for eternity.

To this day the mulberry tree brings forth purple berries.

Old literature has hidden meanings and mythology brings entertaining stories in order to give answers to questions only science can reveal. Lacking scientific knowledge we introduced mythology to answer the unexplained. So much of our world revolves around motive. Fame, fortune, greed and a strong desire to impress others in our society. Mythology revolves around love and power. Although some mythological love stories ended in death, it was an example of the strongest love. To love more than one's self.

Opinions on any given subject vary. If I ask friends about Romeo and Juliet, I would receive many different summaries. There would be an optimistic and pessimistic view. Some would tell me about the feud of their families and others would tell me about young love. It is all about how you interpret what you absorb and the love you experienced.

I just so happen to believe there is a silver lining that surrounds each and every cloud.

> For it was not into my ear you whispered, but into my heart. It was not my lips you kissed, but my soul.
>
> —Judy Garland

Hope

Hope. My favorite word in any language. Hope expresses our expectations of fulfillment and our desires with anticipation.

Optimism in our lives derives from the gift of hope. According to mythology, Pandora gave us the spirit of hope. All mankind enraged Zeus, and Pandora was created as a punishment to men. Pandora was the first woman created and she was sent to Prometheus and Epimetheus. These brothers had only created men and not women.

Pandora was ravishing and was known as "all gifted." She received her gifts from individual gods, and Zeus sent her with a messenger god to Prometheus and Epimetheus. Prometheus did not trust Zeus and warned his brother never to accept gifts from Zeus. Epimetheus disregarded his brother's warning and accepted the maiden. He led the maiden into his home and she followed him with her jar in hand. This jar was sent with her and the gods warned her never to open the jar. The jar was stored with evil from the gods and all the good was given into the making of Pandora.

She was curious and restrained herself from the lid many times, but one moment she decided to let her curiosity end. She opened the lid and black smoke filtered through the air. She frantically tried to put the lid on the jar but the damage had already been done. All the evil was released; she introduced hatred, jealousy, suffering, greed and other evil into the world.

Hope was in the jar and remained until the evil had disappeared from the jar to comfort all in distress.

A spirit of hope expresses our expectations of fulfillment and our desires with anticipation.

> "Don't be content with being average. Average is as close to the bottom as it is to the top."
>
> —Unknown

The Fortune Teller

A warm red glow was in the sky as the sun began to set at the carnival. The rides were just silhouettes against the glow. The carnival had so many pieces of entertainment; music, games and rides. We all agreed on a carnival and always enjoyed every minute. My two youngest sons were eating cotton candy by my side and my two oldest boys were standing and facing a fortune-telling machine the size of a phone booth. The huge magical box contained a mechanical life-sized fortuneteller and she was enclosed in glass along with her magical crystal ball.

The purpose of this piece of entertainment is to give you a fortune card after you deposit a dollar into the machine. You place a dollar in the slot, follow the directions by placing your hand on a small ledge where shown and wait. The cards are preprinted but the sound of the machine working on your fortune sounds authentic. Less than sixty seconds later you have a fortune printed on a 2x3 inch card. It gives you information on your personality, your lucky numbers, your future and other unnecessary information.

The two youngest boys ran to the sides of their older brothers because they needed to see the attraction. I was watching my oldest son and he seemed a bit perturbed. I realized he had a stack of fortune cards in his hands. Each time he received a new card, I watched him read it and shake his head back and forth continuously. He then inserted yet another dollar. Both my older boys had spent their own money and had asked me for a dollar, then another and another....I had to ask: "Why are the both of you collecting these cards? Do we really need so many?" They looked at each other and looked at me as if I should know the answer. After about five seconds, one of the boys exclaimed, "All of these fortunes are **not** mine and I want to try and get mine."

Why should this behavior surprise me? I must keep in mind, these were the same two boys that when ordering Chinese food requested extra fortune cookies. They didn't eat them but they read them. Once again—they couldn't receive the wrong fortune! They knew what they are looking for.

So many thoughts occupied my brain: Two very determined young men, in control and would never settle for any reason. Each boy knew who he was, what he wanted to be and where he wanted to go.

Fortune cards are generic and not so unique.

> "I've never canceled a subscription to a newspaper because of bad cartoons or editorials. If that were the case, I wouldn't have any newspapers or magazines to read."
>
> —Richard Nixon

Media

Media. I try not to view the news on television and avoid it by flipping through the channels and I start reading a newspaper after the first dozen pages of printed news. It would be believed after subjecting yourself to the news for your entire life that you could become immune to all the emotional effects. Media has a special way of bringing forth horrible happenings in the world. Horrendous stories are the first priority and bring forth other's "dirty laundry." It is healthy for me to avoid news because I know I have never excitedly expressed: "Wow, I am so glad I didn't miss today's news!"

The media has brought me news that can alter my emotions. I can feel heartbroken, frustrated or irrational. The only thing that makes me happy is that I am not part of the news!

Media plays the biggest part of any outside influence over society. A writer has an opinion and their writing will tend to favor their judgment. A story is presented with some exaggeration in the favor of the writer. Writers have the ability to give only the facts that benefit their story. Simple rules for reading the news: 1) Read with an open mind; 2) Don't believe everything you read; 3) There's probably more to the story other than what you just read.

One day I skimmed through the newspaper, keeping in mind

that freedom is our country's greatest gift. There was a man (who believed in freedom) holding a sign that read: "Stop Abortion!" Another page had an article about one man accusing another of racism. Still flipping the pages, one headline caught my eye: "The Peace Rally Riots." (Love the irony in the peace rally headline.) As I closed the paper I glanced at the last headline I was to read: "For or Against the Death Penalty?"

When I closed the paper I was only on page eight. My brain was overloaded with information I didn't want to know and shouldn't have read. The news informed me about issues with the absence of taking a stand or having opinions. There was no inclination that the newspaper was for or against abortion, war, racism or the death penalty. They reported only the facts and issues at hand. It is politically safe to maintain a neutral opinion.

No longer are the reporters neutral when they cover a case involving one suspected criminal. The rapist, the thief or the murderer... opinions form and are presented in a reporter's article. Each and every paper has a columnist that clearly states an opinion...one opinion. Theirs. I enjoy challenging opinions of others. I have respect for others as well as their opinion. Only one exception: I recall hearing from a writer: "I've got a gut feeling on this." You can't elaborate on an article on a gut feeling. I had that feeling once. My feeling was that I was to hit the lottery! My gut feeling was wrong.

Television news brings us facts—not opinions—even though the mental anguish is the same result as a newspaper.

I have a friend who explained to me how she was going home to relax. Her plan was to soak in a bubble bath, enjoy a glass of wine and catch the eleven o'clock news. What's wrong with that statement!

MY WORLD: JUMP IN ANYTIME!

I know that I become mentally exhausted when I subject myself to news and avoiding it would be best for me.

The News: Complex drama, chaos and unanswered questions.

My Home: Simple drama, chaos and unanswered questions.

I'll tune out the news and be thankful for the happiness found in simplicity.

I have a collection of media quotes that I found amusing:

> Advertisements contain the only truths to be relied on in a newspaper.
> —Mark Twain

> The hand that rules the press, the radio, the screen and the far-spread magazine rules the country.
> —Learned Hand,
> Memorial service for Justice Brandeis 1942

> The press is the enemy.
> —Richard Nixon

> Journalism is popular, but it is popular mainly as fiction. Life is one world, and life seen in the newspapers is another.
> —G.K. Chesterton,
> *On the Cryptic and the Elliptic*, 1908

> You can never get all the facts from just one newspaper, and unless you have all the facts, you cannot make proper judgments about what is going on.
> —Harry S. Truman, *Mr. Citizen*, 1960

> "Those who hate you don't win unless you hate them, and then you destroy yourself."
>
> —Richard Nixon

Media Influence

"Guilty until proven innocent." Oh, wait…"Innocent until proven guilty." It is unsettling to me and unclear which statement is factual. How do we know what statement is accurate? Can we rectify these statements? Does the media distort, contaminate, corrupt and/or manipulate our thought process?

There are victims of the media circus and I have a name that appears in my mind repeatedly. Robert Durst. He made headlines that implied he was a guilty man before a fair trial. Media has put forth effort to prove a "guilty by association" theory. It is impossible to conduct a trial on hearsay. I'm positive that facts are essential in a trial; unfortunately the media can still assist in creating the opinion of the public. Negative or positive, right or wrong, it is an opinion. The opinion of the media.

Closure. Society wants and needs closure to crimes committed, even if not justified? The accused may not be responsible for the crime, just targeted by reason of association without a motive. The obvious isn't always the obvious answer. We are all victims by convincing ourselves the correct answer by outside influences, and at times we listen to a sentence only to find we may take it out of its context.

Robert Durst, a Manhattan real estate millionaire (possibly billionaire), was burdened with negative spotlight attention due to media exposure for decades. As I place these words upon my paper, he is on trial for "murdering" a neighbor. In a case of self-defense, he is still under attack regardless if he was indeed a victim in this crime.

Privacy is not a word you could find in the Dursts' vocabulary. Robert was only a child when he was exposed to media coverage upon the death of his mother. Decades later, he was haunted by the disappearance of his wife with the media obsessed with the case and the capabilities of sabotage in regard to the Dursts' privacy. Today, another two decades have passed and once again misfortune surrounds him. Remember the old saying: "In the wrong place at the wrong time." Do any of us today give people the benefit of the doubt?

I never pass judgment until I am one hundred percent sure that my decision is based fairly and not altered by others. Accusations are followed by motives. Robert Durst is not shy of accusations. Shy of motives. When I compare to other cases in past history, everyone had a motive. Robert Durst had nothing to gain and everything to lose by committing the crimes he is accused of committing. The media had avoided the question: "Why?" It all goes back to my initial question: "Are you considered innocent or guilty prior to a 'fair' trial?"

As I conclude this segment of my writing, the media once again has interfered with the Durst trial. An undisclosed source gave a Houston television station over one thousand digital photographs that could jeopardize Robert Durst's verdict. KHOU-TV's channel 11 News unhesitatingly made a decision to broadcast those photos to poison minds.

It is frightening to imagine someone's fate is in the hands of the media. Our society has the gift of freedom; freedom of speech, of the press and independent choices. **Think independently.**

Robert Durst was acquitted on November 11, 2003.

"The reason grandparents and grandchildren get along so well is that they have a common enemy."

—Sam Levenson

Golden Rules

The golden rules were guidelines we were given to follow years ago as a child. Do we live by those rules today? I still can hear my mother repeating the quotes that I find myself repeating today:
 "Laughing turns to crying."
 "Treat others the way you want to be treated."
 "Don't make fun of anyone. How would you feel?"
 "We don't hate anyone....We dislike greatly."

I put to use the childish quotes through the years as well.
 "Gotcha last!"
 "You're an Indian giver!"
 "You've got cooties!"
 "Flat-leaver!"

Since 1998 I have written down so many of my favorite segments that have taken place on an ordinary day. Family time together is priceless.

It was a rainy Sunday and we were all held captive inside our home due to bad weather. Everyone tried to keep busy. I considered a day like this a test. It was a day to test your sanity.

Tommy was playing a video game, Casey was on the computer and Vinny and Colby decided to play cards.
Remember their ages: fourteen and five.
Here was the dialogue between the two:
Vince: "Fine. I'll play."
Cole: "Good."
Vince: "Don't cheat."
Cole: "I don't."
Vince: "Your turn, cheater."
Cole: "I'm not a cheater, you are!"
Vince: "Just go and pick a card." (Still grinning)
Cole: "I did."
Vince: "What did you get?"
Cole: "Um, a two and a half."
Vince: "All right, Cole, Tommy is coming in to play with you."
As Vincent starts walking away I hear him laughing: "Two and a half."

> "Fear less, hope more;
> Whine less, breathe more;
> Talk less, say more;
> Hate less, love more;
> And all good things are yours."
>
> —Swedish proverb

A Good Day Is When...

...Four-year-old grasps the concept of **Play-Doh is not a food group**.

...I remember to remove the coffee from the roof of the car—prior to pulling away from the curb.

...A five-year-old realizes that guinea pigs are NOT overweight hamsters.

...A family member sneezes, we all respond with, "God Bless you." We do not respond with either: "Yuck. Cooties." or "Disgusting, you got your germ cells all over me."

...Tommy doesn't remind me that I have 1,341,288,533 minutes to live. (He figures this out by the life expectancy of women and the age I am right now, then breaks it down.)

...A five-year-old stops insisting that he has zeros in his name.

...I say: "I'm broke." It doesn't mean my money is broken and I can fix it.

...One of my children asks me a question that I am able to answer. (This reassures me that my brain waves are still functioning.) Then again John J. Plomp was the one who said: "You know that children are growing up when they start asking questions that have answers."

...Each and every person has their own perspective on various issues in their lives. Involved subjects to the uncomplicated everyday situations are interpreted through individual eyes.

...An impeccable illustration: A child of mine loves to wear team jerseys. He explained that the reason he promotes the last place team. "You never have expectations of winning and you won't be disappointed when you lose." He truly has his own perspective when sports becomes a topic of conversation.

...Another example: I was eating at a restaurant when I heard screaming. A child just began his tantrum. Numerous people in the vicinity of my table appeared to be annoyed and aggravated. Not me. I just ignored it. My friend wanted to know if I heard all the noise pollution in the restaurant. I responded: "Listen, I am so glad that it is not my kid, I don't care. Let him scream."

All in perspective.

Living with opportunity to learn.
Experience allows me to grow.
To be who I am.
What I was intended to be.

—Susan Thomas Alexandria

"The tragedy of life is not that it ends so soon, but that we wait so long to begin it."

—W. M. Lewis

Printed in the United States
21275LVS00001B/229-276